Making Period Dolls'
House Accessories

Making Period Dolls' House Accessories

Andrea Barham

Guild of Master Craftsman Publications Ltd

First published 1996 by
Guild of Master Craftsman Publications Ltd,
166 High Street, Lewes,
East Sussex BN7 1XU

© Andrea Barham 1996

ISBN 1 86108 014 X

Photography © Andrew Barham 1996

Illustrations © David Crawley 1996

Cover by Ian Hunt Design 1996

Designed by Fineline Studios

Typeface: New Aster

Origination in Singapore under the supervision
of MRM Graphics

Printed in the UK by the University Press,
Cambridge

For Rebecca, Jessica, Elliott, Emma, Isobelle and Adam

Acknowledgements

Grateful thanks go to my father David Crawley
for working so hard on the illustrations; to my
husband Andy Barham for the exacting
photography; to my editor Lindy Dunlop for
all her care and attention to detail (a woman
after my own heart); and to Liz Inman for all
her encouragement.

Measurements

Although care has been taken to ensure that metric measurements are true and accurate, they are only conversions from imperial. Throughout the book instances will be found where an imperial measurement has fractionally varying metric equivalents (or vice versa), usually within 0.5mm either way. This is because in each particular case the *closest* metric equivalent has been given, so that a measurement *fractionally* smaller will be rounded down to the nearest 0.5mm, and fractionally greater will be rounded up. (*See also* the Metric Conversion Table, page 155.)

Patterns and templates are actual size and may be directly traced for use.

Finding Suppliers

To locate stockists and suppliers of the materials referred to in this book, please consult your local telephone directory or the many excellent magazines available, for example:

British	American
Hobby's Annual	Miniature Gazette
Hobbies (Dereham) Ltd	Miniature Showcase
Panduro Hobby Catalogue	Fibreworks Publications
Dolls' House World	Nutshell News
Dolls' House and Miniature Scene	The Catalogue of Dollhouses, Supplies and Miniatures
Janet Cole's Beads	Ornament
Earring Things (The Bead Merchant)	Jewelry Crafts
Popular Crafts	American Craft
Practical Crafts	B.R. Artcraft Company

Contents

Introduction

In Ann Ruble's book, *Through the Looking Glass: Collections in Miniature*, she suggests an interest in collecting is something one may be born with. This concept struck a chord with me since I have been fascinated by miniatures and collecting for as long as I can remember. I consider myself extremely fortunate to have a whole industry that has grown up to complement my lifelong passion.

I am a collector by nature along with many people who have a similar passion for collecting items such as teapots, postcards, plants. ... There is clearly much satisfaction to be gained from building up a unique collection; but what to do with all the plates, stamps or cat ornaments once you've acquired them? I think for me that is the attraction of the dolls' house: the contents of a huge household scaled down to fit into the corner of one room. There are precious few quality antique miniature articles to hunt down so they can quite legitimately be reproduced by the enthusiastic amateur.

The advantage of home-made collectables is that the possibilities are endless and there's practically no expense involved once you've built up a collection of basic raw materials. I like to appropriate materials from other people's hobbies, such as filigree findings from egg crafting; thin wood strip, metal tubing and belaying pins (these look like tiny lace bobbins) from model shipbuilding; findings and beads from bead suppliers; tiny metal alloy figures from war games suppliers; buttons, bric-a-brac and linen from charity shops; miniature mouldings from dolls' house shops; and bits and pieces from florists, cake decorators and haberdashers. It's also gratifying to make use of fascinating and intricate natural objects such as feathers, cones, flowers, shells and even a sloughed-off snake skin. I also have an ever-increasing collection of magazine clippings ready to be transformed into miniature works of art.

If you're new to the interest, don't feel daunted if miniature work strikes you as very fiddly. It is. Everyone finds it so. If your results aren't all you'd like them to be perhaps you are working too fast. One point well worth bearing in mind is, just because a thing is small it doesn't mean it's going to be quick to make. That's why a handcrafted miniature collectable can cost much the same as its full-size equivalent – just as much work goes into making it. Every stage of work must be given its appropriate share of time even if this means putting it away and coming back to it later; a method which can suit some people very well. The time factor was brought home to me some time ago as I watched a needle-woman who had become quadraplegic, continue her passion for embroidery with the aid of a specially designed apparatus which allowed her to sew using her teeth. This necessity made the task much more laborious but the end result was superb.

Incidentally, there is no need to feel guilty about indulging in close work. Even in a bad light it does no permanent damage to the eyes themselves. It might however fatigue the tiny muscles surrounding them which may cause a temporary headache. A magnifying glass can sometimes be useful, if you have less than perfect eyesight. You really can't beat natural daylight or failing that use a daylight bulb.

I prefer to work in the traditional scale of an inch to a foot (1/12). However, if you prefer, some of the projects could be adapted to a smaller scale. My miniatures are rarely faithful reproductions, more an amalgam of the gist of a few examples of the full-size article. I refer to my second-hand copies of *Miller's Antique Price Guide* for dates and technical terms, as I find it helps to know a little about the objects before attempting to reproduce them. Social history in the form of other people's experiences is fascinating. Don't feel you have to stick rigidly to one particular style or period for your room settings – mixing a variety of styles can create a more natural and personal effect.

CHAPTER ONE

Tools and Materials

Tools

Listed here are the tools I find most useful. Most of them are generally available and don't need specialist skills.

Junior fret saw Ensure the cutting edge bites on the forward stroke.

Small thin-nosed pliers Found in hardware stores and bead suppliers' catalogues.

Small snips Use for cutting wire.

Household scissors For cutting fabric and paper.

Power scissors These are similar to kitchen scissors, have a serrated blade, and cut through most things.

Manicure or embroidery scissors You will need good quality, sharp ones.

Pins and pin cushion Dressmakers' pins, T-pins and darning needles are useful to position things and apply glue.

Tweezers Useful for picking up tiny components.

A sharp craft knife Changeable blades are preferable.

Fine sandpaper and heavy duty emery boards Emery boards are less likely to round off edges than sandpaper.

A polishing and sanding stick This is useful for getting into awkward corners. Available from hobby shops.

Small round file Useful for enlarging thread holes in findings or beads.

Rubber bands Use these for holding glued parts together while they dry.

Mitre block This enables right angles to be cut into beading and mouldings. A small plastic one will do.

Jig I use a jig to hold an assembly in a fixed position while the glue dries.

Pencil Use this for marking wood and tracing patterns.

Eraser Always use a soft, clean eraser.

Metal rule I use this for cutting and scoring.

Metric and imperial rule I use one with a $\frac{1}{16}$ calibration.

A tiny vice I have mine screwed to a worktop.

A small pin vice or electric mini drill and tiny drill bits Useful size tiny drill bits are: $\frac{1}{32}$ and $\frac{1}{16}$in (1 and 1.5mm). When working with an electric drill, always wear safety goggles.

The smallest drill bits are the most likely to snap. If this should happen the project can still be finished using a strong, sharp dressmakers' pin as a bit.

Set of modelling tools These are easily found in hobby shops, but you can improvise your own, e.g. skewers and pinheads.

Tube benders These are tubes of closely coiled metal which will bend a metal tube without crimping it.

Small G-cramps and bulldog clips Useful for clamping drying parts together.

Masking tape Handy for masking off certain areas when spray painting.

Tracing paper or greaseproof paper Use these for tracing patterns.

Squared paper I use this for making patterns.

Fig 1.1 An old filing cabinet is useful for storing tools and materials

Adhesives

All your miniatures will benefit from using the right adhesive, correctly applied. Below is a list of the adhesives I have used in the projects, together with details of how to use them.

PVC glue This is an all-purpose glue, also known as R/C modellers' craft glue, which dries clear. I call it tacky glue.

Instant bond glue Known generally as superglue. The multi-bond type, superglue 4, will stick most things. Read instructions before use. It can be reinforced with jewellers' cement, available from craft shops.

If you get superglue on your fingers, separate them gently using thin card, and rub the area with a little nail varnish remover.

Wood glue Specialized wood glue makes a solid bond once dry.

Glass glue Loctite is an example of a glass glue, useful for glass-to-glass or glass-to-metal bonds. It only cures in ultraviolet light (sunlight). Read instructions carefully before use.

Epoxy resin Two-part resins, such as Araldite Rapid, need to be blended together. Use sparingly and wipe away excess before it dries. It can discolour brass over time.

Double-sided tape Useful for sticking leather or thick fabric. It also allows for repositioning, if you change your mind.

Spray mount Hangs giftwrap wallpaper and some fabrics. It allows for repositioning, but becomes permanent over time. Always use in a well-ventilated area.

Blu-Tack Useful for temporary joins, however, it can leave a mark on some wallpaper or fabric if used to hang pictures.

Grip Wax A specialist adhesive which is useful for sticking ornaments or pictures to shelves or walls without looking obvious or staining. Available from dolls' house suppliers.

Scatter Grip This stays tacky but does not dry so it can be useful to temporarily secure ornaments very unobtrusively. Available from dolls' house suppliers.

Silicone sealant This is normally used as a bathroom sealant. It is useful for insulating bare wires when fixing 12 volt electrics in a dolls' house. Simply smear it on and leave to dry.

Keep a small bottle of surgical spirit handy. It often helps to wipe some over surfaces before applying glue, to remove any dust or oil residue.

Fig 1.2 A selection of useful adhesives

Paints

Acrylics These are fast drying, water-based paints. They are easy to use and brushes can be washed out in water. For good results, it is worth investing in some good quality fine paintbrushes. For a shiny finish use an acrylic varnish or spray with clear lacquer.

Oils For a good metallic finish use oil-based paints. Thick and thin solvent-based silver and gold marker pens are a useful alternative to tins of paint. You may want to invest in a small tin of brass oil paint since this colour doesn't come in pen form. Oil-based paints take 24 hours to dry.

Fig 1.3 Various metallic spray paints and marker pens

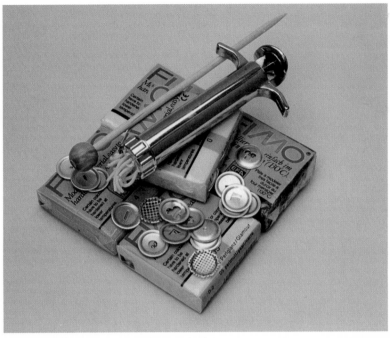

Fig 1.4 Fimo, extruder, and improvised modelling tool

Fibre-tipped felt pens Fine felt pens can be used in the same way as fine paint brushes. Dot colour on until you build up the effect required.
Spray paints Cellulose car spray paint is the most economical way to buy spray paint. The primer and clear lacquer are useful too. Spray piece inside a cardboard box in a well-ventilated place.

Cans of gold and silver spray paint are often discounted after Christmas.

Modelling Compounds

Fimo I tend to use Fimo modelling material but there are other brands such as Sculpty and Formello, which are widely available. These are similar to Plasticine, but will harden permanently in a conventional oven. Any shade can be blended from red, yellow, blue,

brown, black, white and transparent, as you would mix paints. Always blend darker into lighter shades, using tiny amounts.

If a piece of Fimo has become too soft from blending, put it in a cool place for a while. Conversely, speed up blending by placing hard blocks of Fimo over a gentle warmth such as a radiator.

Choose a suitable work surface and use a light touch so your fingerprints don't show. Keep your hands clean and free from fluff, especially with white Fimo. Use modelling tools, available from craft shops, or whatever comes to hand for texturing.

Harden Fimo in a conventional oven from 210–270°F (100–130°C) for 10–15 minutes. The residual oven heat after cooking is often sufficient to harden miniature models. This is referred to as a cooling oven in the projects. Check that the temperature isn't too hot by using the thermostat set at the appropriate temperature.

Once hardened your model is ready to be painted, varnished, drilled, filled or added to. If your Fimo work breaks, don't panic, it can usually be glued back together with superglue.

Epoxy putty Milliput is the best known brand. The regular colour is a yellow/grey. Use Superfine white for a porcelain effect and terracotta for earthenware. It is a two-part epoxy putty which must be blended together. It can be used as a modelling compound or as a joining compound. It hardens in about three hours, but the process can be speeded up with heat. Small amounts will harden more quickly. Once hardened it has similar properties to Fimo. If you find Milliput too pliant to model, leave it to harden for a while.

Stains and Varnishes

Wood stain Spirit-based wood stains can be mixed together or thinned with white spirit. Light Oak and Georgian Medium Oak are two I use frequently. Strong solutions of tea or coffee make a subtle alternative.

Varnish I prefer the finish of French polish to that of varnish on furniture. It can be brushed on like regular varnish, applying several thin coats. Button polish is similar, but more orange in colour. Shellac is a thicker version which can be thinned.

French polish jars can be notoriously difficult to open. Wind a thick rubber band tightly round the lid for a better grip and open while wearing a rubber glove.

Spray lacquer and clear nail varnish Spray lacquer is useful for spraying a thin coating onto small accessories. It protects painted furniture and silver-plated or copper accessories from tarnishing. Nail varnish is a cheap alternative and comes with its own brush.

Varnish stripper Brands containing dichloromethane need to be scoured off. Products such as Ronstrip Peel-Off, containing sodium

Fig 1.5 Various wood preparations

hydroxide, take longer to act but *can* be peeled off. Always read the instructions carefully and be sure to wear protective clothing, goggles and gloves when using varnish stripper.

Danish oil and wax furniture polish Danish oil can be rubbed into wood with a cloth (after staining) in the form of an oily polish. Danish oil followed by wax furniture polish gives a good finish for seventeenth century furniture or older, giving a more authentic aged look than any applied varnish. It is especially important to get a smooth finish on the bare wood before application.

Finishing Materials

Spray starch Use to make fabric look authentically draped. Spray liberally onto fabric, shape into folds or as required, and leave to dry.

Transfer medium There are several of these available, for example Decal-it, Super Sealer, Mod Podge. They will convert magazine clippings into custom-made transfers. Apply in thin coats. Mod Podge comes in matt and gloss. Each product comes with instructions, but here is my method, specifically for miniatures.

METHOD

1 Cut out clipping, with a ½in (12.5mm) border.
2 Tape edge of clipping to a flat surface and apply six to eight thin coats of transfer emulsion onto right side, allowing each coat to dry before applying next. (If picture starts to fog, don't apply any further coats.)
3 Leave transfer to cure for two hours.
4 Soak in warm water for a further two hours, then remove backing by gently rubbing it with your finger.
5 The transfer should be almost transparent. If there is any dried paper still on the back, soak transfer again.

6 Carefully trim transfer with manicure scissors. Stick your finished transfer where you want it – the emulsion will act as a glue.

Silver plating solution Intended to re-plate worn, full-size silverware. It will plate many base metals such as copper, brass, and some gilt and nickel. Plate any small components before assembling, as any glue residue will prevent plating. If you have difficulty getting a plated item to stick, use Araldite.

Components

Finding components for your miniatures is a matter of always being on the look out for interesting bits and pieces and recognising their potential – if not now, in the future. Make a habit of not discarding anything which might have a use.

Charity shops, jumble sales, flea markets, car-boot sales, market stalls, hardware shops, florists, hobby and craft shops are some useful sources for bits and pieces to make your

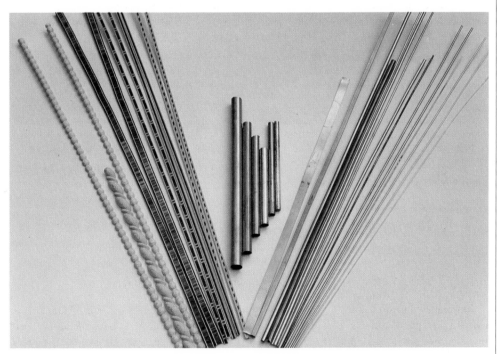

Fig 1.6 A selection of wood and metal strip and tubing

accessories. Specialist magazines and mail order suppliers are also useful for certain DIY components. Some accessories require particular special components – details of where to find these are given with individual projects. Listed below are some materials I like to have to hand. The list is not exhaustive, and there are often suitable alternatives to the parts I have used.

Metals

Brass tubing (¹⁄₁₆ and ³⁄₃₂in (1.5 and 2.5mm) are especially useful)

Copper and aluminium tubing

Solid brass rod (¹⁄₃₂ and ¹⁄₁₆in (1 and 1.5mm) are useful sizes)

Brass strip

Thin copper or brass sheet

Tiny brass nails, ¹⁄₃₂in (1mm) (from dolls' house suppliers)

Hardware components such as brass screw-eyes and eyelets

Thin brass and nickel fuse wire and beading wire

Wood

Thin strips and sheets of wood (from mail order suppliers)

Turned components such as banister spindles and belaying pins (from dolls' house suppliers)

Miniature mouldings, skirting, cornice and picture frames (from mail order suppliers)

Thin wood veneer, such as microwood (from mail order suppliers)

Wooden dowels, skewers, cocktail sticks, orangewood manicure sticks (orange sticks), lolly sticks and corks

Small wood offcuts

Jewellery Findings and Beads

Jewellery findings (it is sometimes cheaper to buy old necklaces and unstring them for beads and findings)

Gilt, plated, and nickel jewellery findings

Trace chains

Fig 1.7 Build up a collection of decorative wooden beads and buttons

> Order trace chains from mail order bead suppliers. Avoid curb chains since they look rather modern and the individual links are curved and thus useless. When collecting broken chains to re-use, look for the finest ones.

Decorative beads: wooden, plastic, china and glass (mail order catalogues are a good source of specialist beads such as bugle beads (glass tubes), rocaille beads (known as seed beads) and rhinestones (tiny imitation jewels)

Decorative filigrees (from egg crafting suppliers)

Old brooches, earrings and fancy buckles

Electrical Components

Micro bulbs with fine wires, 12 volt

Candle-shaped micro bulbs (from dolls' house suppliers)

Fabrics and Haberdashery

Natural fabrics with small prints (small bundles of printed fabrics are sometimes sold for making patchwork quilting)

Narrow and wide embroidered braid (sewing shops and market stalls)

Suitable curtain fabric (can be used for upholstery fabric)

Thin, cheap, sewing thread (ideal for miniature needlework)

Buttons, preferably glass and wooden ones,

Fig 1.8 Fabric with small patterns is excellent for making miniatures

Fig 1.9 Embroidered braid can be used for soft furnishings and upholstery

though plastic are also effective (look in charity shops)

Embroidery silks

Felt

Old glove leather

Hook and eye fasteners

Found Objects

These items will be found by chance and it is best to build up a collection of useful looking components to have to hand.

Linen handkerchiefs

Small cotton doilies

Small ornaments and souvenirs

Table mats and runners (useful as carpets and rugs)

Magazine clippings (these often show items in a tiny size, just right for dolls' house accessories, and can be used to make transfers)

Cheap brass miniatures

Plastic novelties (Christmas cracker novelties, once primed and painted, can be effective)

Cake decorations

Old plastic containers and lids (lipstick cases and make-up trays can be useful for certain accessories)

Fig 1.10 Table mats and runners can be put to good use as carpets and rugs

Fig 1.11 Cake decorations can be customized for making miniatures

CHAPTER TWO

Decorative Techniques

Wall Coverings

Specialist dolls' house shops and mail order suppliers stock an ever-increasing selection of miniature wallpapers. However, if you're prepared to search a little further afield you might prefer these cost-effective alternatives – they give a satisfying degree of individuality to your room settings.

Fig 2.1 Full-size wallpaper suitable for miniature decorating

Fig 2.2 Hunt around for good quality wrapping paper in gift shops

Full-Size Wallpaper

Avoid the ultimate economy of papering your dolls' house with leftover oddments from your full-size decorating projects – it will look out of scale.

Browsing around DIY shops is one of my favourite pastimes. There are always plenty of tools, paints and components to ponder over and many large DIY shops are happy to provide a small sample of wallpaper to try before you buy. Not that I'm suggesting you help yourself to samples with no intention of making a purchase – heaven forbid. From time to time I happen upon full-size wallpaper I fall in love with and redecorate a room that doesn't need redecorating.

For period settings I favour paper wallpaper rather than vinyl. Vinyl gives a modern plastic sheen which can destroy the period illusion. Avoid textured papers, with the exception of Anaglypta (plain raised patterns) which can be used as plaster moulding below a dado or chair rail.

Large, bold wallpaper patterns can be very effective in a Victorian setting, e.g. bold florals. Green wallpaper was considered a restful shade for the Victorian bedroom but it had unfortunate side effects for the unsuspecting occupant. The green pigment in the newly discovered aniline dyes contained arsenic. The vapours weren't lethal, but they did tend to make the victim feel rather unwell. Arsenic poisoning from green wallpaper is reputed to have contributed to Napoleon's demise.

Giftwrap Wallpaper

Keep a look out for suitably patterned wrapping paper. Avoid shiny or poor quality papers as they are problematic to hang and show every minor flaw or defect. Don't go shopping for wallpaper with a particular colour scheme in mind, start a collection. Buy any giftwrap with potential, roll it up and store it away in a cardboard tube. The ultimately unsuitable sheets won't go to waste; they can always be used to wrap up presents!

Fig 2.3 A great variety of materials can be used effectively for floor coverings

Victorian Scraps

Victorian scraps – consisting largely of little children, kittens and roses – can be used to make a nursery border. Trim the scraps neatly and stick in a random, overlapping fashion just below chair rail height. Once dry, apply a thin coat of French polish to give an aged effect. Neaten the top edge by fitting a chair or dado rail, available from dolls' house suppliers, to the wall.

Use standard wallpaper paste to hang giftwrap and wallpaper but be careful – it contains fungicide which reacts with copper tape laid below and can show through green. I prefer to paste the paper onto thin card and stick this to the wall over the tape.

Mouldings such as cornices and skirting need fixing to walls. I suggest using a glue such as Balsa or Polystyrene Cement rather than wood glue since with them the fixtures can be easily prised off if you change your mind.

Fabric

Back in the sixteenth century tapestries were used as much to keep out the draughts as for decorating walls. Georgians were far more likely to use fabric rather than paper for wall coverings. Make a collection of fabrics suitable for wall coverings. Charity shops are a good source for small pieces. Boldly striped shirt fabric can make an effective Georgian or Regency wall covering. Silk (or a synthetic alternative) is suitable and can be hung using spray mount.

A weak solution of food colouring can be used to tint the fabric. I have used a wall covering in a Georgian sitting room which was an offcut from my mother's wedding dress. I soaked it in food colouring (yellow with a spot of blue).

Floor Coverings

A wealthy Elizabethan household might own expensive woven rugs from the East, but these were too precious to be stepped on – they were draped over walls and tables. During this period, woven rush matting replaced the loose rush floor covering of the mediaeval house. A full-size rush tablemat makes excellent floor matting. Odd tablemats can often be picked up in charity shops for a few pence. Simply pick out and discard any gold decorative thread with a large pin.

During the seventeenth century parquet flooring became fashionable and was sometimes protected with a covering of straw.

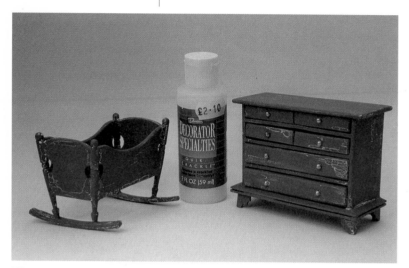

Fig 2.4 An instant ageing effect can be achieved with Quik-Crackle

Waxed, kitchen shelf-lining paper with a suitable pattern, mounted on thin card, makes excellent linoleum. Look for it in hardware stores. A linoleum-look can also be achieved by applying a few even coats of transfer emulsion to giftwrap or wallpaper and mounting on card. Sticky-back plastic is available, but tends to lift and become sticky over time. Full-size mock granite or small-patterned linoleum sample squares can also be effective.

If possible, I prefer to use authentic materials. Slabs of slate cut to size make an attractive kitchen floor. My pieces of slate have been collected over time. A good place to look for small pieces of broken slate is your local churchyard.

If you don't want to spend time cutting up and laying Microwood veneer parquet strips (sticky-back wood strips), improve dolls' house parquet floor paper by coating it with transfer emulsion along the grain to give texture and sheen.

Parquet was still in use during the eighteenth century when carpets were at last allowed onto the floor. Velvet or velveteen will make a plain pile carpet. A simple patterned carpet can be made with a flock product such as Floc-Kote, spray mount and templates. More intricate patterns can be carefully penned (I prefer to work with solvent-based felt-tip pens) onto thick pile velvet of a pale colour. Ensure each colour dries completely to avoid smudging. Carpets were bordered at this time.

Packs of ⅜ x ¹⁄₁₆in (10 x 2mm), second quality pine strips make ideal and economical floor boardings. These can be stained and polished or 'limed' (scrub on a dilute grey emulsion) for the bedroom and nursery.

Floorcloth, or oilcloth as it was sometimes known, was extensively used. To make floorcloth paint heavy linen with oil-based paints. Floorcloth was cheap and practical and continued into the latter half of the nineteenth century when it was replaced by hardwearing and hygienic linoleum (a mixture of cork and oil on a cloth base).

Distressing

For period decor to appear authentic the conditions of the day must be taken into account. Burning candles left sooty marks on walls, as did oil and gas lighting, and coal heating. Soot marks can be simulated with black acrylic paint. Matt black spray paint gives a good sooty effect if sprayed in a spurt.

Wallpaper once hung can be painted with lemon juice to discolour it slightly. Avoid paint or paper containing our modern preference for brilliant white. To counteract blue whiteners in paint, add a dot of orange which opposes it in the colour spectrum. Add oil paint to solvent-based paint and acrylic to emulsion.

A deteriorated look can add wonderful atmosphere to an attic, lumber room, disused nursery or servants' quarters. A very effective aged appearance can be achieved by a complete beginner with ageing products, such as Quik-Crackle, available from craft shops. Here is the method I use.

METHOD

1 Paint the surface to be treated with an off-white base coat of acrylic and allow to dry.

2 Liberally paint on Quik-Crackle in selected

places, feathering strokes to blend in.

3 Leave to dry for about 20 minutes, then immediately brush a darker colour all over. This coat will instantly crack in the places where the Quik-Crackle was applied.

4 For a gloss finish to furniture, spray with clear lacquer when dry.

This technique is great fun to use on furniture, walls, or any surface with a painted finish.

Pleating

Nowadays there are specialist mini-pleaters designed for miniaturists. Whatever happened to that good old fashioned alternative, corrugated cardboard? It's not quite so evident as it used to be, but it's still about if you look for it. It is often used as packing for glass bottles, and is sandwiched between card in some cardboard boxes.

Here's a simple way to make your own pleater at no cost. Have a heavy book to hand.

Fig 2.5 A home-made pleater

METHOD

1 Cut two pieces of corrugated cardboard long enough to make full-length curtains.

2 Thread a bamboo skewer into each corrugation to make it more ridged.

3 Saturate fabric with spray starch (hair spray can be used if you're in a hurry as it dries more quickly.)

4 Lay fabric over one pleater so there is some overhang to one side, about 5in (127mm). Place second pleater over the top. Wiggle them together until the corrugations fit into each other.

5 Hold top pleater lightly with your free hand, use other hand to press your knuckles firmly across the centre, towards the fabric overhang. The pleater should 'eat in' the excess fabric as you press. Repeat at both ends of the pleater and again at the centre. Now do similarly for the two remaining areas either side of the centre. Finish by running your knuckles randomly across the

top of the pleater to ensure all excess fabric is pulled in.

6 Weight down with a heavy book. Once completely dry, carefully peel the fabric away without disturbing the pleats.

Use different size corrugations to make different width pleats.

Materials

Corrugated card

Bamboo skewers

Spray starch

Fabric

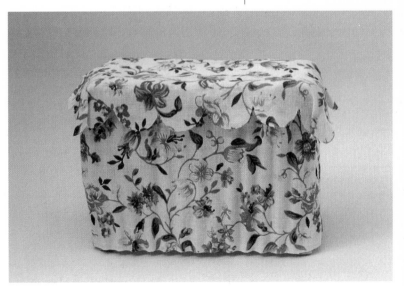

Fig 2.6 Pleated table covering

CHAPTER THREE

Customizing Furniture

Fig 3.1 Right: original chair; centre: painted table; left: painted chair and cushions

Victorian Garden Furniture

There is an ever-increasing selection of affordable dolls' house furniture available, often in sets, which can be customized to suit your preferred style or period.

This white metal furniture, sometimes found in gift shops or at car-boot sales, makes excellent Victorian garden furniture. It looks even more convincing when sprayed dark green.

METHOD

1 Prime table and chairs, and spray green with several thin coats.
2 Use wide braid to make cushions. Cut a template to make sure they are all the same size. Tuck the excess in and stitch together by oversewing sides together. Stuff lightly with cotton wool.
3 Sew ties of thin ribbon to cushions and tie to chairs.

Materials

Metal table and chairs

Car spray paint: Peugeot Forest Green

Wide braid

Narrow ribbon

Cotton wool

Materials

Metal chaise longue

Spray paint: gold

Thin packing foam

Fabric

Decorative trim for edging

Tassels

Cotton wool

Fig 3.2 Original chaise longue

Fig 3.3 Customized chaise longue

Chaise Longue

The beauty of white metal furniture is its versatility. A simple coat of paint can produce a very different look, and the use of different fabrics and trimmings can transform a piece. I have dressed up this chaise longue to resemble the richness of eighteenth century furniture.

METHOD

1 Spray chaise with several thin coats of gold paint.
2 Cut a length of thin packing foam to fit seat. Cover foam with fabric, sewing back, top and bottom seams.
3 Lash cushion to seat with needle and thread.
4 Pin and sew edging over seam to neaten.
5 Fray a length of fabric to make a fringe. Glue to underside of chair.
6 Sew a tube of fabric to make round cushion. Gather one end and secure with a knot. Turn out. Stuff with cotton wool. Gather open end.
7 Sew a tassel to the centre of each end.

Fig 3.4 Left: original chair; right: customized leather chair

Materials

Embossed Spanish souvenir purse or wallet

Cheap chair

Thin marker pen: gold

Thin packing foam

Tacky glue

Embossed Leather Chair

This project will make good use of that souvenir purse from Spain, masquerading as leather, but usually embossed card. If you don't have one, look in your local charity shop where you'll find them in pristine condition in abundance.

The original chair belongs to the Victoria and Albert Museum, London and dates back to around 1720. Made in walnut, the embossed blue leather seat cover is gilded (highlighted in gold).

Fig 3.5 Leather articles from charity shops, including embossed Spanish purse

METHOD

1 Mark out sufficient piece of purse to cover the seat with an overlap for the edge. (I trimmed the chair down to fit remaining length by cutting a little from the top with power scissors.)

2 Cut a length of thin packing foam to fit seat. Cover foam with leather and glue in place on chair. Trim excess leather.

3 Glue leather to back of seat.

4 Decorate raised pattern with gold marker pen or rub with a cream wax metallic finish.

Materials

Wide upholstery braid, 1.5ft (45.7cm)

Snippet of matching fringe

Snippet of matching cord

Very thin packing foam

Card, e.g. greetings card

Tacky glue

Side Chair

The chair below the upholstery came out of a very cheap set which didn't merit repolishing. I covered it with wide upholstery braid with something like a William Morris style pattern – and nobody likes it but me.

METHOD

1 Glue thin packing foam onto card. Cut and glue to fit chair back and seat.
2 Drape braid from the legs over the back and seat to the other side. Choose where to place pattern and pin braid to the foam.

Although it's quicker, I don't recommend using glue on fabric, as it can spoil the finished effect. Use a needle and thread where possible, and try to keep stitching hidden.

---

3 Turn in braid edges at the two sides of chair back and pin. Lash sides together

Fig 3.6 Customized side chair

with a needle and thread, keeping the stitching hidden.
4 Cut two side pieces from the braid which fit in the gaps between legs, allowing for seams.
5 Turn in edges and pin to the main cover.
6 Lash side pieces to the main piece.
7 Tie a tight knot in the cord. Fray the short end and trim.
8 Stitch cord to back seam of chair to help disguise join.
9 Repeat for other side.
10 Trim fringe to an appropriate length and stitch to the base of chair.

To age fabric, either soak in a weak solution of black tea for a moment or, as I did here, rub over with dressmakers' chalk or dust with a layer of talcum powder. Brush off excess.

Fig 3.7 Upholstery braid is available in many patterns

Fig 3.8 Original desk (before removing mirror) and chair

Materials

Milliput

Spray primer: white

Car spray paint: Volkswagen pastel white

Marker pen: gold

Acrylic paint: black

Pearlized beads

Small gilt shells (optional)

Hook and eye fasteners

Small brass nails

Fabric: gold patterned

Superglue

Georgian Ivory and Gilt Desk and Chair

These two pieces did not start life together, as you can tell from the picture. I removed the mirror from the dressing table by snapping it off, and prised off the cushion seat.

METHOD

1 Remove original knobs and fill holes with Milliput.

2 Sand down and spray on several thin coats of white primer.

3 Spray with a few coats of Volkswagen pastel white. This colour is ideal as an antique white.

4 Gild the set with a thin gold marker pen. (I also stuck on some small gilt shells to decorate the desk and chair legs.) Dull the gilt a little with a black acrylic wash made from diluted black acrylic paint.

5 Since it is a writing desk, I decided to put it on casters. These are small, pearlized beads,

glued to the base of the legs and painted gold.

6 Use large hooks from hook and eye fasteners. Pull hooks apart a little with pliers and stick a tiny ball of Milliput to handle curve. Press it flat. Paint the handles gold and fix them into the drawer using small brass nails.

7 In place of stuffing, use Fimo (or Milliput) shaped to appear well used, to give an antique impression.

8 Shape and harden the Fimo then cover it with a piece of gold, patterned fabric.

Fig 3.9 Customized ivory and gilt writing desk and chair

CHAPTER FOUR

Ladies' Accessories

Moth Balls

The crystals used in this project are salt crystals sold in hardware shops as water softeners, or dishwasher salt. Sort through the salt for some of the larger crystals.

METHOD

1 Chase crystals around an egg cup with the purple felt-tip pen until they are all coloured.
2 Cut a circle of lint, put crystals in centre and tie up with thread. Trim to neaten.

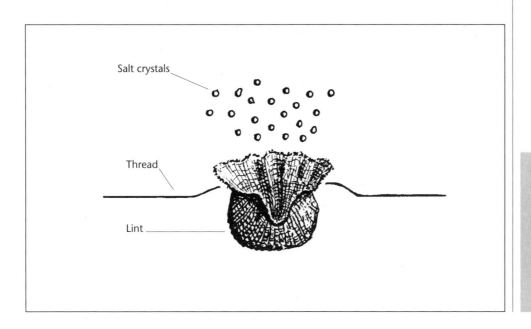

Salt crystals

Thread

Lint

Materials

Salt crystals

Snippet of fine lint

Snippet of thread

Felt-tip pen: purple

23

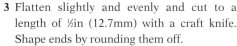

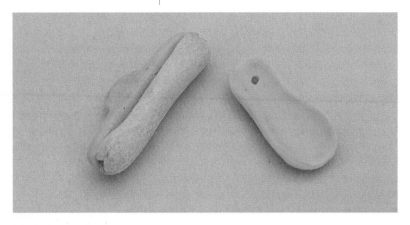

3 Flatten slightly and evenly and cut to a length of ½in (12.7mm) with a craft knife. Shape ends by rounding them off.

4 Blend in a small, flat semicircle of Fimo for the handle with a pinhead. Harden in a cooling oven.

5 Trim a section of white leather slightly wider than the buffer and ⅝in (15.9mm) long. Spread with glue on the wrong side and roll up as tightly as possible.

Old, worn gloves can often be found in charity shops. Soft glove leather is just the right thickness for miniatures.

---

6 Glue the seam of the leather roll to the underside of the buffer. Trim the ends at an angle so they can be turned up and glued onto the buffer as well.

SHOEHORN

1 Roll a pea-sized ball of ivory Fimo into an oval and flatten to 1/16in (1.6mm) thick.

2 Place onto a metal cylinder former that can withstand heat, e.g. a thick brass rod. This will give the shoehorn the appropriate curve.

3 Shape top of shoehorn with a craft knife and smooth.

4 Make a small hole in top half of shoehorn with a pin. Harden in a cooling oven, still on former. Wait until Fimo is completely cold before removing from former.

Materials

Fimo: white and yellow

Thin white glove leather

Tacky glue

Nail Buffer and Shoehorn

As a natural way to shine nails, the nail buffer was used until the advent of cosmetic nail lacquers in the twentieth century. This miniature buffer is a working model.

METHOD

BUFFER

1 Mix a scrap of yellow Fimo with a small amount of white to make ivory.

2 Roll a thin, even sausage of ivory Fimo about ⅛in (3.2mm) thick.

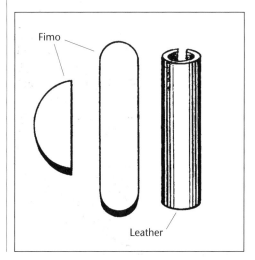

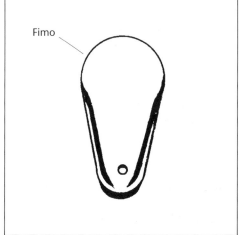

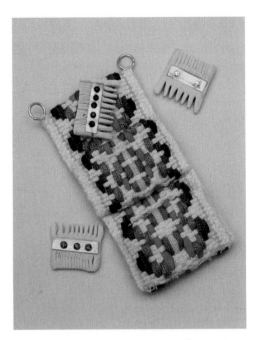

2 Squeeze a slight waist into the short sides.

3 Gently flatten onto a baking tray. Using a craft knife, cut close indentations along one long edge for close-set teeth.

4 Do likewise on the other side, but cut teeth much wider, tapering to a point. (Don't worry too much how these teeth look at this point.)

5 Press a strip of brass, cut to size, across the centre. Harden in a cooling oven for 10 minutes.

6 While still warm, trim both comb ends into a slight curve with manicure scissors.

7 When cool, very gently sand large teeth to regular points.

8 Carefully drill a few indentations along the brass strip using a ½in (1mm) drill bit.

> The comb will be too fragile to clamp into a vice. Use Blu-Tack to secure it to a scrap of wood to hold it steady.

9 Glue tiny rhinestones into holes to decorate.

Materials

Fimo: white and yellow

Thin brass strip

Small jump rings x 2

Embroidered braid, preferably cotton

Tiny rhinestones

Tacky glue

Combs and Case

This bone and brass comb was modelled on one I saw in an engraving of a Danish bedchamber dated 1645. Similar ones were used in the fourteenth century and date all the way back to the Pharaohs. This one must have been a particularly fine specimen, set with rich jewels. The case hung by a looking glass.

METHOD

CASE

1 Fold over end of braid and hem. Sew a jump ring to each hemmed corner.

2 Trim to about 2in (5cm), then turn a small hem onto the right side at the bottom.

3 Turn top of a second short length of braid under, and hem. Turn bottom under and sew onto end of backing strip (right side out). Repeat for second pocket, placing it centrally.

COMBS

1 Mix a speck of yellow with a little white Fimo to make bone colour. Flatten a small pea-sized ball into a rough square. Pull out to form a rectangle.

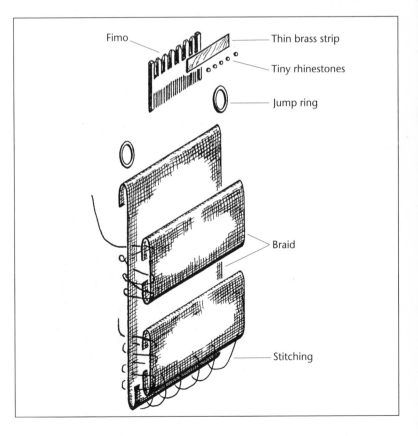

Fimo — Thin brass strip — Tiny rhinestones — Jump ring — Braid — Stitching

Materials

Medium silver/nickel spiral cage stone mount

Thick silver wire, ½in (1mm)

Hook from a large hook and eye fastener

Wired micro bulb, 12 volt

Fimo: black and red

Acrylic paint: black

Nail polish: red

Araldite

Brazier and Curling Tongs

The fashionable sixteenth century lady curled her hair into ringlets, using curling tongs heated in a coal brazier. During the mid-seventeenth century Mrs Samuel Pepys appears to have put the tongs to a more unconventional use by drawing back her errant husband's bed curtains and brandishing them at him.

A large, straightened hook and eye hook will serve for the tongs. It is worth looking in your local charity shop, at the bottom of the button box, to see if you can find a lovely old rusty one. They are often brass or iron.

The silver spiral cage stone mount is a jewellery finding used to hold a gemstone. It's available from bead and finding suppliers.

METHOD

BRAZIER

1 Grasp one end of spiral cage with pliers. Twist to uncoil top a little. Clip small top coil under the mid-coil so that it catches and stays in place. This acts as the tong holder.
2 Cut five lengths of silver wire and bend to the shape shown for legs.
3 Push base of coil into a pyramid of Blu-Tack

to hold it firm. Apply Araldite to the two contact points on leg and place inside brazier using tweezers.

Allow each leg to dry before applying the next, otherwise they slide and knock each other over.

---

4 Repeat with four remaining legs, evenly spaced. You may need to adjust or trim legs so the brazier stands up straight.
5 Wash over with dilute black acrylic, to age.

COALS

1 Paint bulb with red nail polish. When dry, thread bulb wires through coil at base.
2 Chip small pieces from a cold block of black Fimo to make coal. Make a few similar pieces in red. Harden in a cooling oven.
3 Spray coals with spray mount and arrange over bulb in brazier, red coals to the centre. Be sure to arrange a few coals to cover the bulb.

When installing the brazier, thread bulb wires through table covering to hide the electrical connection.

TONGS

1 Straighten old iron hook from large hook and eye fastener with pliers. Old hooks and eyes were more simply made than our modern counterparts, but are more difficult to straighten with pliers. (If using a modern hook, snip off a straight edge from two unbent hooks, then glue together.)

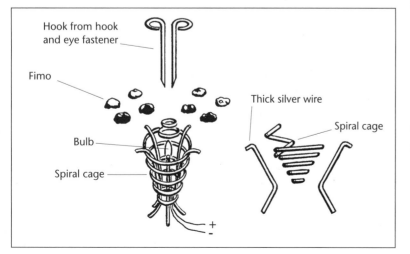

Hook from hook and eye fastener

Fimo

Bulb

Spiral cage

Thick silver wire

Spiral cage

Spiral cage

+

Silk Shoes

For this project I customized some cheap plastic dolls' shoes. (These are often sold in sets, as shown in the photograph.) Each shoe needs to measure 1in (25.5mm) or less. To make a 1920s pair, I added a Cuban heel of Milliput. Trim shoes with bows, rosettes or buckles where appropriate.

Recently one of my seventeenth century shoes became inadvertently distressed – it went up the Hoover. I liked the effect so I popped the other one into the bag as well then gave them both a good dusting off with a stiff paintbrush.

METHOD

COVERING SHOES

1 Pare off any bow or buckle patterns from shoes as well as any unwanted lumps or bumps with a craft knife.
2 Adapt shoe to suit chosen period, e.g. pare down heel, or build up into a Cuban heel using Milliput, and leave to harden.
3 Spray shoe with spray mount, or spread very thinly with tacky glue.
4 Cut a horseshoe shape from silk, larger than shoe, with a slit down the centre. (*See* illustration.) Press base of horseshoe onto toe of shoe.
5 Stroke and press remaining silk around sides of shoe.

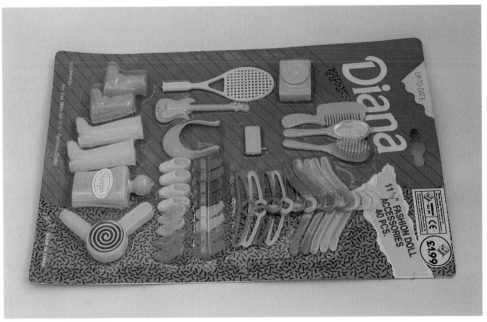

Fig 4.1 Plastic dolls' accessories

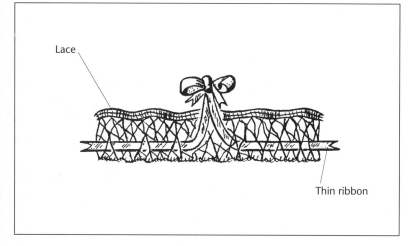

Lace

Thin ribbon

piece of silk. Stick the centre of the fabric to the centre of the inside of the heel horizontally. Fold the rest around heel, trim excess with manicure scissors and press round to join up with first part.

SOLE AND INNER SOLE

1 Glue a snippet of scraped-down leather to the sole to cover silk ends. Trim to size with manicure scissors.

If possible, use a craft knife to scrape away as much backing from the leather as you can, to cut down on bulk.

---

2 Cut an inner sole from thin leather or suede. Glue inside shoe.
3 Repeat above method for second shoe.

BUCKLES

1 For buckles use tiny flat chain links with a snippet of thin brass rod glued to the centre.

BOWS

1 Tie a tiny bow with the two ends of a length of thin ribbon. Snip the bow from the ribbon length leaving a short length at the ends.
2 Position the bow in the centre of a snippet of holey lace. Thread the ends through the lace, gather and sew to edge of shoe.

6 Trim silk, then press one side to the back. Fold a tiny seam with the other side and glue down over first piece.
7 Cut two nicks in silk overlap to allow silk to fold inside shoe. Press until it sticks. Pay special attention to neatly folding back seam inside.
8 Trim excess silk to a few millimetres. Fold and glue onto the heel and sole.

HEEL

1 Use a separate snippet of silk to cover the heel, or use the excess lower silk, trimmed to size. Fold over and glue a small seam in a

Materials

Pair of tiny plastic dolls' shoes

Scraps of silk

Snippet of thin leather

Scraps of trimming

Chain links

Snippet of brass rod

Milliput

Spray mount or tacky glue

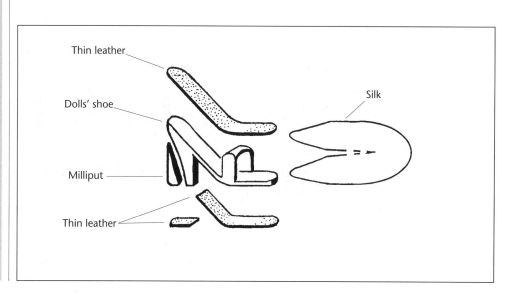

Thin leather

Dolls' shoe

Milliput

Thin leather

Silk

CHAPTER FIVE

Gentlemen's Accessories

Materials

Ball and hook earring stud

Jump ring, ³⁄₁₆in (4mm)

Trace chain

Tiny link

Tiny watch face clipping, e.g. from magazine or catalogue

Snippet of thick fuse wire

Tacky glue

Araldite

Silver Pocket Watch

You'll need a ball and hook earring stud finding for this project. These have one flat half and one concave half, with a loop underneath. Use nickel or silver-plated components. Gilt will make a gold watch. I used old findings for mine. If new ones look too shiny, wash over with a dilute black acrylic paint to give them an antique appearance.

METHOD

1 To make case, snip off post of earring stud as close to the back as possible with power scissors. Sand smooth. Gently and carefully prise open to make a right angle.

> **Don't overstress the hinge, or the ball will break into two pieces.**

2 Glue jump ring centrally over watch face clipping with tacky glue. Trim clipping to size. Glue face onto concave half of case.
3 Attach trace chain to loop on case with a tiny link.
4 Glue a snippet of straight, thick fuse wire to top link of trace chain with Araldite.

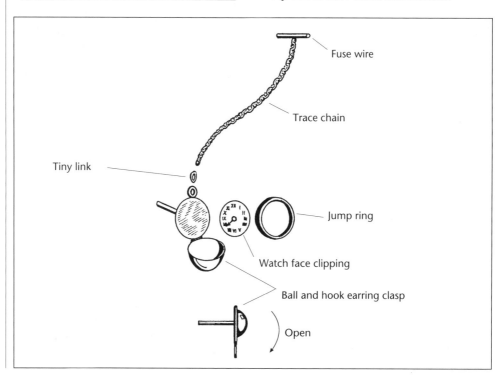

Fuse wire

Trace chain

Tiny link

Jump ring

Watch face clipping

Ball and hook earring clasp

Open

Meissen Desk Stand

This stand is based on a Georgian design of 1750, with ink in the lidded pot and sand to dry the ink in the pierced pot. The pots are both removable. The quills were kept in the taller holder. If you know someone with a budgie, certain budgie feathers make ideal quills. Don't worry, you won't have to pluck any, they moult quite naturally. Alternatively, suitable feathers are available in craft and hobby shops.

METHOD

STAND

1 Thoroughly wash and dry the eye shadow tin. Firmly grip a corner with thin-nosed pliers and bend it towards the centre just a little. Crimp edges either side of the bend, and bend outwards a little to flute the edge. Repeat on three remaining corners.

2 Cut pierced spacer in half centrally with a junior hacksaw. Sand rough edges. Arrange on stand, together with medium pierced bell cap. Glue in place.

> I find superglue's invisible quality when dry ideal for gluing metal findings which are to be primed and painted. The priming and painting process helps to cement the joint.

INKWELL

1 Bend rim of eyelet up slightly. Glue eyelet to inside of deep bell cap.

2 Glue gold bead to thread hole of medium plain bell cap.

SANDER

1 Bend rim of eyelet up slightly. Glue to inside of deep bell cap.

2 Glue small pierced bell cap over eyelet, domed side up.

QUILL STAND

1 Glue washer over thread hole of pierced bell cap, which was glued to base earlier.

2 Bend rim of eyelet up slightly. Glue to inside of deep bell cap. Glue assembly to washer on stand.

Materials

Feathers x 2

Large rectangular metal eye shadow tin (empty)

Large pierced spacer

Medium pierced bell cap

Plain deep bell caps x 3

Medium eyelets x 3

Small pierced bell caps x 2

Small washer

Medium plain bell cap

Tiny gold bead

Superglue

Spray primer: white

Fine solvent-based felt-tip pens: blue and gold

Clear lacquer or polish

3 Glue small pierced bell cap over eyelet, domed side down.

DECORATION

1 Spray stand and pots with four or five thin coats of white primer, allowing to dry in between each coat.

White spray car primer gives an excellent unfired porcelain effect – a fine, matt, slightly textured finish. If you suspect you are sensitive to spray paint, it is well worth investing in a cartridge respirator, available from DIY shops.

---

2 Once dry, trace around the sander, galleries, holes in shaker and quill stand with blue felt-tip pen.

3 The original inkstand was decorated with scattered *'Deutsche Blumen'*. I simply scribbled a few rose-like blooms on the base and pots.

Keep the blue decoration simple. When painting a design, find something to copy, and practise a little first. It is possible to white out the odd slip of the pen with white acrylic, but wait until it's dry first as this can get a bit messy.

---

4 Meissen porcelain was often gilded so I decided to add a little gilding with a fine gold pen. Leave to dry for 24 hours.

5 Once dry, spray with two thin coats of clear lacquer or, alternatively, coat thinly with iridescent clear polish. This gives a most convincing glazed effect.

It is imperative that the stand is completely dry before applying the lacquer. If the decoration is coated or sprayed too early it will run and smudge and you will have a Meissen reject.

---

6 Stick quills into stand.

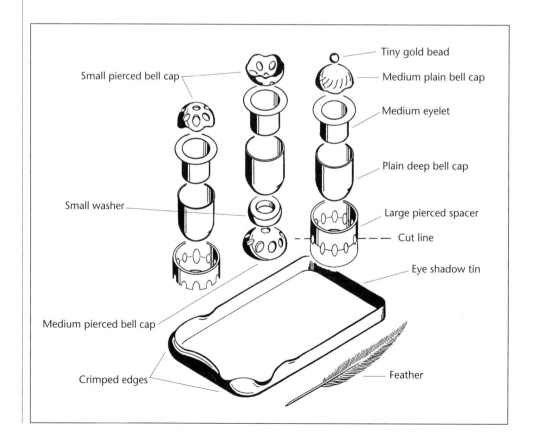

Small pierced bell cap

Tiny gold bead

Medium plain bell cap

Medium eyelet

Plain deep bell cap

Small washer

Large pierced spacer

Cut line

Eye shadow tin

Medium pierced bell cap

Crimped edges

Feather

Materials

Round-topped torch bulb

Small glass seed bead

Large glass seed beads x 2

Large flat-backed faceted crystal

Small flat-backed faceted crystal

Large glass bead: brown

Brass eyelet

Gilt trace chain

Eye from small hook and eye fastener

Watch back or brooch mount

Glass glue

Grip Wax

Milliput

Clear brown varnish

Brandy Decanter and Glass

I always wondered what use those spent torch bulbs could be put to, and then I had the idea to make this delightful decanter and brandy glass.

METHOD

DECANTER

1 Glue eyelet over thread hole of large glass bead with glass glue.
2 Glue large seed bead to flat-backed crystal to make stopper. Attach to decanter with Grip Wax.

NAMEPLATE

1 Fill the centre of the eye from hook and eye fastener with a little Milliput and smooth flat. Once hardened, paint eye and Milliput gold and leave to dry.
2 Attach the chain to thread holes of the eye. Drape nameplate over neck of decanter.

BRANDY GLASS

1 Pinch off the metal screw end of the torch bulb with pliers.

Occasionally a bulb will shatter, so wear gloves and work with the bulb inside a clear plastic bag.

---

2 Carefully nibble off glass down to the bulbous end with power scissors. The rim will still be jagged at this stage.
3 Very gently and carefully stroke the bulb over medium fine sandpaper until the rim is smooth.

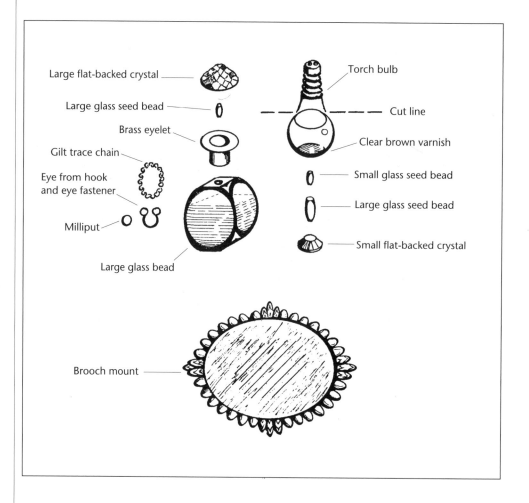

Large flat-backed crystal

Large glass seed bead

Brass eyelet

Gilt trace chain

Eye from hook and eye fastener

Milliput

Large glass bead

Torch bulb

Cut line

Clear brown varnish

Small glass seed bead

Large glass seed bead

Small flat-backed crystal

Brooch mount

Sanding the bulb takes a while – save it for when you're engrossed in the television. This part can take a minute or two if you use a mini drill with the finest grinding stone. Apply the bulb to the stone with even pressure but don't use any force. Always wear protective gloves and goggles while working with a mini drill.

---

4 Finally, smooth any remaining burrs gently with a very fine, round metal file. As soon as you get a good result, stop! These bulbs shatter easily if too much pressure is applied or the grade of sandpaper is too coarse.

5 Centre and glue remaining large seed bead onto small, flat-backed crystal using glass glue. Glue small seed bead on top of this. Finally centre and glue bulb onto above assembly.

You might need to scrape the silvered backing off the flat-backed crystal if you can't find a clear one. The backing scrapes off quite easily with a sharp craft knife.

---

6 To make brandy, drop several drips of brown varnish into the glass, allowing each to dry. Swill the last one or two around the glass before it dries.

TRAY

1 Attach glass and decanter to brooch mount or watch back with Grip Wax.

Ship in a Case

Order the smallest metal alloy ship stocked by a war games supplier (suppliers are listed in War Games magazines.) I used a two-masted brig in the 1/1,200 scale Napoleonic warship range. Unfortunately the ship didn't come with assembly instructions. What I know about rigging a ship could be written on a sequin so I puzzled it out with the help of the model ship section of a craft and hobby magazine.

METHOD

SHIP
1 Paint all parts of the ship (I chose brown for the wooden bits and cream for the fabric bits.) Assemble with superglue when paint is dry.
2 Use manicure scissors and tweezers to add rigging. Paint a length of beading wire off-white. Cut to required size, dip both ends in tacky glue and position on ship, for rigging.

Materials

Metal alloy model ship

Thin beading wire

Clear acrylic sheeting (Butyrate)

Thin wood strip (or matchsticks)

Thin wood veneer

Snippet of brass strip (not shown in illustration)

Thin adhesive lead strip, retailed for full-size lead lighting (optional)

Tacky glue

Wood stain

Superglue

Acrylic paints: white, brown and cream

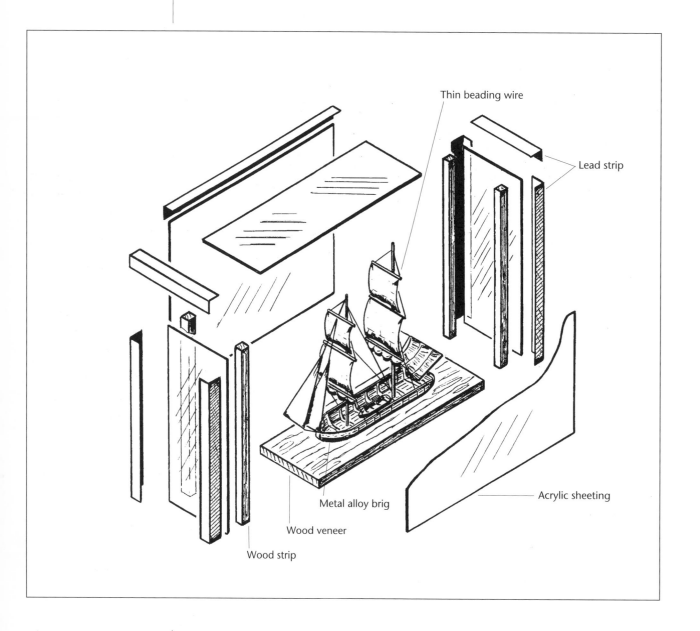

Thin beading wire

Lead strip

Acrylic sheeting

Metal alloy brig

Wood veneer

Wood strip

CASE

1 Measure length and height of ship, add ⅛in (3.2mm), and cut two rectangles this size from acrylic sheet. Lightly sand edges. Repeat above process for width and height of ship.

2 Fit the four pieces of acrylic together to make a case with no lid or base. Cut four wood strips to fit each corner, and stain.

3 Glue the acrylic sides and corner strips into a box with no base or lid using tacky glue.

4 Cut a rectangle from the wood veneer sheet to fit the base of the case using power scissors. Glue ship onto base. Glue case over base and ship.

5 Cut a piece of acrylic to fit as a lid using power scissors. Glue into place.

6 Edge the corners of the case with adhesive lead strip.

7 Glue a tiny brass strip to the front of the case as a nameplate (not shown in illustration).

Silver Wax Jack

This wax jack is a copy of a Georgian original which dates back to 1798. The wax taper – similar to a thin candle – was coiled around the rod and threaded through the hole at the top, where it was lit. The melted wax was used to seal correspondence. The wax itself was usually lampblack or vermilion (bright red). All wax jack components should be silver-plated, or nickel.

METHOD

WAX JACK

1 Glue small, thin washer to tiny eyelet, broad side down. Bend thick silver wire into shape shown using pliers. Glue opposite sides to either side of eyelet, washer on top.
2 Glue earring clutch to button, broad side down, to make base. Fix above assembly to base with a small ball of Milliput. Once hardened, paint silver.
3 To make rod, bend a small loop in one end of a length of thick wire.

If you want a short cut, use the straightened section of a suitably sized hook from a hook and eye fastener.

---

4 Fill small end of conical finding with Milliput and press end of chain inside with a pin.
5 Attach other end to loop on rod using tiny link.
6 Thread pointed end of rod through link nearest cone. Measure against stand and snip rod to size.

SEALING WAX

1 Blend a speck of red Fimo with a tiny amount of transparent Fimo. Roll into a thin string.
2 Coil Fimo twice around rod leaving a little extra length. Place in a cooling oven to harden.
3 Pinch off end of wax and glue to lower half of tiny eyelet. Glue a short length of wax to top of washer, as if wax were threaded through hole.
4 To assemble wax jack, lay stand on a little salt or similar to support it and glue rod holding wax horizontally across stand with Araldite.

Superglue is quicker to use, but may not be quite so durable on silver-plated components. If you choose to use Araldite, squeeze two lines of each glue into a piece of scrap paper, then just mix together a little at a time with a toothpick or cocktail stick. The glue will not start to harden until it is mixed.

Materials

Small thin washer

Tiny eyelet

Thick silver beading or fuse wire

Large hook from hook and eye fastener

Earring clutch

Thin metal button

Trace chain

Cone finding

Fimo: transparent and red or black

Milliput

Araldite

Marker pen or acrylic paint: silver

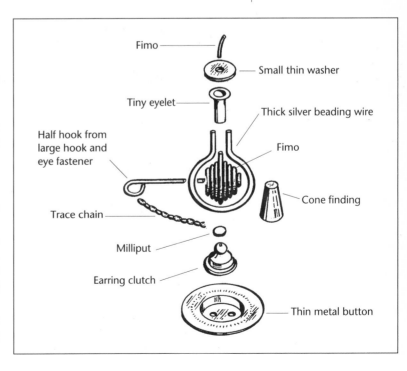

Leather-Bound Volumes

These leather-bound volumes take a while to make, but are most impressive when scattered about the library. You will need a fat jotter pad, the type bound with a strip of white glue along the back edge. Find a cheap one, since the sheets are usually thinner. White pages are only appropriate for modern books. Green, pale blue, pale yellow, grey and buff make good period books. I left the pages of this book blank, but apparently, Sir Arthur Conan Doyle personally wrote a miniature Sherlock Holmes Mystery for Queen Mary's Dolls' house in a book of similar size.

I've had a tiny novelty Bible in gilt and mother-of-pearl since I was about ten. They are still available today. I clipped it together with a bulldog clip, removed the staple, and re-bound it with a liberal application of tacky glue, then proceeded with the method below.

METHOD

PAGES

1 If the books are to go into a bookcase, first determine the appropriate size. Mark the dimensions onto the jotter with a pencil, close to the bound edge. Mark out the number of books required. Split the pad to an appropriate thickness for the size of book.

2 Using a metal rule and a sharp craft knife, carefully score across the width of the jotter (sides of books) till it comes away from the rest of the pages. (Clip the leftovers back together and put them back by the phone!)

When making a set of volumes, complete each step for all the books at once. If you make them singly they never quite seem to match.

---

3 Score down the jotter to divide each book at the pencil mark. The most difficult part is cutting the books to an even, regular size. It is worth spending a little time cutting them evenly.

I take the precaution of wearing old leather gloves when scoring with a craft knife. The knife should be sharp: an accident is much more likely to happen with a blunt knife because force is needed to make a cut.

---

4 Clamp pages into a large bulldog clip and stroke a marker pen over the three edges

Materials

Soft glove leather

Jotter pad

Thin cord, e.g. crochet cord (not shown in illustration)

Thin card, e.g. shirt backing card

Snippet of lace (not shown in illustration)

Thin gold twine

Tacky glue

Felt-tip pens: various colours

Thin marker pen: gold

Spray paint: gold

without the glue binding. Be mean with the paint – too much colour seeping between the pages will stick them together. Page edges can be coloured with gold, silver, red or blue. Leave to dry for 24 hours if using solvent-based metallics. For a delicate yellowed effect squeeze the excess liquid from a used tea bag and stroke it along the book edges.

HARDBACK COVERS

1 Lay book onto one edge of card. Pencil around outline. Square up the lines with a set square and cut out two pieces of identical card for every book. The card should be a shade larger all around than the exact size of the book.
2 Repeat above for book spines, one for each book. The height of the spines should match the height of the hard covers.
3 Smooth a little tacky glue onto the thin cord to stiffen it. Glue the cord to the book spine, to resemble tooling (decorative indentations). The simplest decoration is to put two horizontal lines across the top and one at the base.

LEATHER BINDING

1 Lay leather suede side up on flat surface. Smear covers and spine of book with a thin coat of tacky glue. Place front cover onto leather, then spine, then back cover. Fold into a closed book shape before glue dries.
2 Cut away excess leather, leaving a small margin around the outside of the hard covers. Glue this overlap to the inside covers. Trim and neaten the corners carefully, applying a little more glue if necessary, with a pinhead.
3 Fix the set of pages in the cover by gluing the first and last pages over the inside of the hardback cover. This covers the leather overlap, and stands as end papers.

HEADBANDS

1 Poke a little glue down either side of the top of the spine. Snip off a short length of thin gold twine and poke one end into either side. Press down with a pin.

DECORATIVE TOOLING

1 When the books are finished, hold them together with an elastic band and, using a rule,

run the thin gold marker pen lightly over all the tooling so it will appear level on the shelf.
2 It's also fun to add gold decoration to the cover using a stencil. Cut a paper template a little larger than the book cover. Fold the template in quarters and cut out a pattern to suit a snippet of lace, e.g. a diamond-shaped piece. Glue the template over the lace. Place a protective sheet of paper under the book cover. Place the template over the cover and spray very sparingly with gold paint. Remove the template to reveal fine gold tooling.

Practise using a stencil on a scrap of leather first. Gold spray paint is impossible to remove if you make a mistake.

---

3 A variety of lace will give different effects. An attractive effect can be made with a thin strip of lattice lace made into a template and placed round the edges.
4 A decorative stamp can be made for the spine by using a screw winder from an earring back, pressed into a little gold paint.

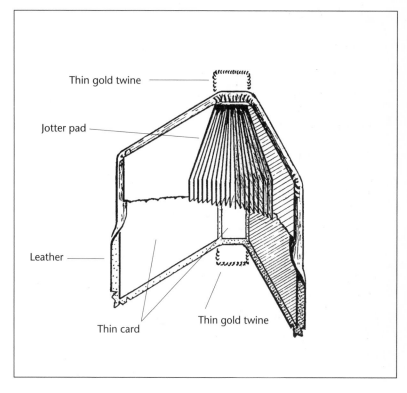

Thin gold twine

Jotter pad

Leather

Thin card

Thin gold twine

CHAPTER SIX

Travelling
Accessories

Walking Sticks

Walking sticks are appropriate for any period setting. They can range from the simple rustic to the sophisticated gentleman's stick with an integral spirit flask.

Rustic Stick

METHOD

1 Search out a suitable T-shaped section of twig. Trim to size so that the off-shoot makes the stick and the main shoot makes the handle. Leave to dry out.

A good source of tiny twisted twigs is a well established climbing plant. I found plenty to choose from on a Russian vine.

---

2 Sand lightly and apply a few coats of French polish.

Gentleman's Stick

METHOD

1 Sort out a tiny glass bugle bead or ampoule end which fits into a ³⁄₃₂in (2.5mm) metal tube, to stand for a spirit flask. (I have also used a suitably straight twig with the centre drilled out.)
2 Cut brass tube to size, about 2¼in (57mm), paint black or brown and varnish.
3 Fit an eyelet over the top end of the stick for decoration.
4 If the ampoule top is too long, sand it down lightly. If using a bugle bead, seal the end with a dot of superglue.
5 To hold the base of the ampoule or bugle bead upright, fix in some Blu-Tack. Drip in a drop of nail polish or French polish to represent liquor.
6 Thread a medium crystal bead followed by a seed bead onto a dressmakers' pin, for the stopper. Secure with glass glue. Trim pin to size.
7 Seal flask by gluing stopper into flask with

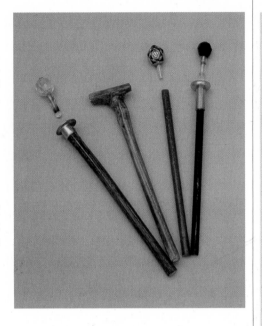

glass glue.
8 Carefully place flask and stopper into hollow of tube or stick.

Don't be tempted to push the flask into the tube or stick too firmly. Thin glass is very fragile.

Materials

T-shaped twig

Metal tube/wood stick, ³⁄₃₂in (2.5mm)

Eyelet or tube and washer, ⅛in (3mm)

Crystal beads or similar

Tiny glass seed bead

Tiny glass bugle bead or ampoule end

Dressmakers' pin

Acrylic paint: black and brown

French polish

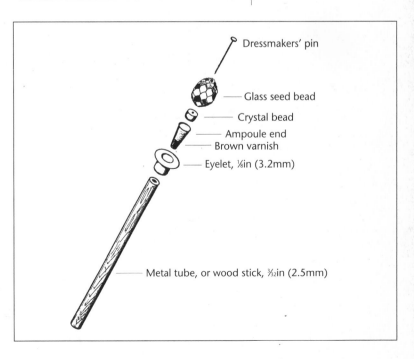

Dressmakers' pin

Glass seed bead

Crystal bead

Ampoule end
Brown varnish

Eyelet, ⅛in (3.2mm)

Metal tube, or wood stick, ³⁄₃₂in (2.5mm)

Felt Hats

To make a hat, a piece of felt is damped down, treated, and pulled over a 'block', or former, to form the shape. Felt hats were popular with men of the mid-nineteenth century in the form of the hard bowler hat. The homburg, a softer alternative, was popularized by the Prince of Wales (later to become Edward VII). Bowler hats were usually black but could also be brown or fawn. Ladies wore hats of straw, velvet or silk until the twentieth century, when they too adopted felt hats such as the 1920s bell-shaped cloche hat.

Materials

Thin felt, various colours

Spray starch

Water-based varnish or transfer emulsion, e.g. Decal-it

Trimming

Dressmakers' pins

Seed beads

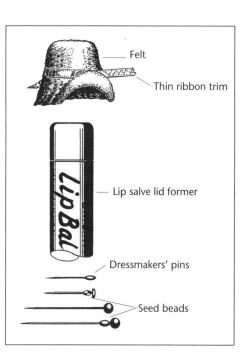

Felt

Thin ribbon trim

Lip salve lid former

Dressmakers' pins

Seed beads

METHOD

HAT FORMER

1 Find a suitable shape to use as a hat former. I used the rounded-off lid of a lip salve tube but anything about 2in (51mm) in circumference can be used. Try small bottle caps, beads on sticks, or lipstick cases.

A hat former can always be custom-made from modelling material, e.g. Milliput.

SOFT HAT

1 Saturate felt with spray starch.
2 Pull felt tautly over former, secure with a thick rubber band and leave until dry. Tie a knot in the band rather than wrap it around the hat, to avoid making ridges in the felt.
3 Once dry remove from former. If a brim is required carefully press the edge flat with a cool iron. Trim to shape with manicure scissors.

BOWLER HAT

1 Saturate felt with a water-based varnish medium.
2 Pull felt over former and leave until dry. Varnish or emulsion will appear white at this stage, though it will dry clear.
3 Once dry remove from former and press edge flat to make brim, with a cool iron. Trim to shape with manicure scissors.
4 Gently but firmly press the bowler hat base onto the surface of a standing iron to roll brim slightly. Don't burn yourself!

DECORATION

1 Make hatbands from narrow ribbon or soutache (a plain woven braid.) I usually prefer to sew decoration on but a dot of tacky glue will do the job.
2 Feathers can be curled in much the same way as curling paper, by running the quill lightly over a scissor blade.

Always trim the bottom of a feather rather than the top.

---

3 To make hat pins, thread seed beads onto dressmakers' pins and secure with superglue.

Handbag

Handbags came into vogue in the 1920s and 1930s. With no pockets, a girl had to have somewhere to put her lipstick.

METHOD

1 Trace pattern shown in illustration below and cut out in leather. Fold along vertical lines onto wrong side and glue down. (*See* view.)
2 Fold along horizontal lines to form a bag shape. (*See* view.) Lightly glue the side pleats together, incorporating the base pleat. Hold the sides until they stick.
3 Fold the flap over. Snip a tiny slit in the centre of the flap. Sew a bead onto the bag so it can fit through the slit as a fastening.
4 Cut a strip of leather 4 x ⅛in (102 x 3.2mm) for the strap. Glue ends together to make a band.
5 Glue strap join to inside of bag.

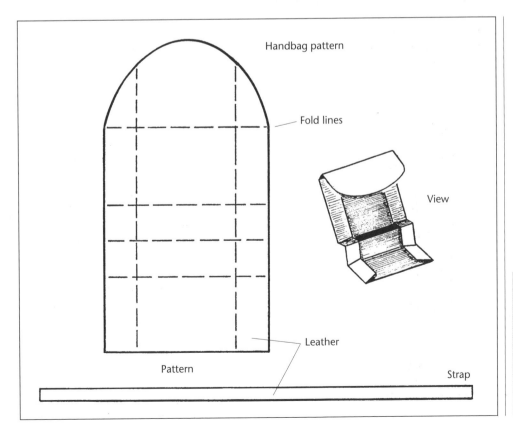

Handbag pattern

Fold lines

View

Pattern

Leather

Strap

Materials

Soft glove leather

Small bead (not illustrated)

Tacky glue

Materials

⅙in (1.5mm) thin
wood sheet

Small rectangular
metal eye shadow tin
(empty)

Fretwork from
wooden fan

Wired micro bulb,
12 volt

Charred breadcrumbs
or similar

Foot Warmer

In the 1600s foot warmers were housed in a wooden box and were used regularly indoors as well as when travelling. In later centuries brass and earthenware foot warmers and, of course, rubber hot water bottles appeared. The design for my foot warmer is copied from a painting by the Dutch artist, Gabriel Metsu, from the 1660s. I found the wooden fretwork fan in a charity shop.

METHOD

1 Make up a rectangular wood surround with a height of ½in (12.7mm) and no base or lid, to house the eye shadow tin snugly.

2 Stain two sections of fretwork fan and glue together (the wood is very thin). Cut a rectangle of fretwork to fit into top of box, sand edges and glue in place.

Any pierced material can be used in place of a fretwork fan. Simply drill a pattern of holes through thin wood sheet.

---

3 Cut a base in wood sheet, slightly larger than the box. Stain base and box.

4 Glue tin centrally onto base with Araldite. Check box cover fits neatly over the tin.

5 Drill a tiny hole through both box base and tin. Thread bulb wires through hole. Surround bulb with charred breadcrumbs. (Alternatively, use black and red Fimo to make coals, or use black and red beads.)

If you clean the toaster out regularly, you may be out of luck here. Along with a mountain of crumbs in mine I discovered tiny coals in the form of large, well charred breadcrumbs.

---

6 Thread bulb wires from foot warmer under floorboards when connecting to electrical circuit.

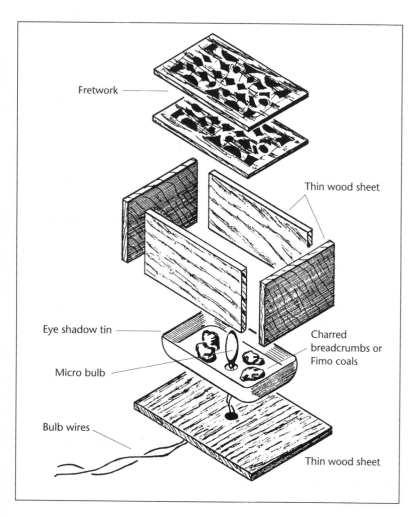

Fretwork

Thin wood sheet

Eye shadow tin

Charred breadcrumbs or Fimo coals

Micro bulb

Bulb wires

Thin wood sheet

Umbrella

By the end of the eighteenth century umbrellas were a common fashion accessory. A miniature tartan umbrella is most effective. For this I used thin tartan ribbon, often found tied around Christmas cakes, rather than haberdashery ribbon.

I recently noticed the workings of a cocktail umbrella and decided it might be fun to try and make a working umbrella. As you can see from the illustration it turned out to be quite straightforward. I made the first using two strong jump rings. The second has two tiny eight hole bell caps as central fixings.

METHOD

1 Spray fabric with starch, smooth and cut out a circle of 3¼in (82.5mm) diameter. (I drew around a drink coaster as a template.)

If using wide ribbon, gather one side tightly to make a pleated circle of fabric.

2 Cut eight spokes, 1½in (38.1mm) long, from thin brass rod. Bend one end of each spoke securely over the jump ring or bell cap using fine pliers (or blunt manicure scissors).

When choosing links and jump rings for this project, choose strong ones. If removing from a chain, cut and discard the adjoining links so the chosen links retain their strength.

3 Cut eight lengths ¹⁵⁄₁₆in (23.8mm) long, from thin brass rod. Join these to the second jump ring (or second bell cap) by bending ends, as over page.

4 Bend the opposite end of these rods over the eight tiny oval links in a similar manner.

5 Thread the bamboo skewer or brass rod (sharpen one end of brass rod with sandpaper) through both jump rings (or bell caps), with the attached hooks facing towards the handle end. Ensure spokes are

evenly spaced, then push the skewer point through the dead centre of the fabric circle. Stick point lightly into Blu-Tack to support structure while you complete the next step.

6 Bow (bend) each spoke slightly and thread each into the oval link attached to the shorter rods. Once all are threaded, arrange spokes evenly in a fully open position, by pushing the second jump ring (or bell cap) down to meet the first.

7 Glue a tiny seed bead to end of each spoke with superglue.

8 Sew a length of thread through the oval link and fabric, knot and tie off. Trim thread ends and apply a tiny dot of tacky glue to secure knot inside. Repeat for opposite spoke. Continue securing the spokes which are at right angles and finish with the intermediate spokes.

9 Pull the fabric tautly to end of each spoke. Oversew a tiny stitch through the fabric, across the spoke. Apply a tiny dot of superglue to the bead at end of spoke and to the stitch, to hold it taut when umbrella is open. Repeat for opposite spoke, then

Materials

Thin material, e.g. silk

Brass rod, 0.02in

Thin ribbon or braid trim (not shown in illustration)

Tiny seed beads x 8

Tiny oval links x 8

Strong jump rings, ³⁄₁₆in (4.5mm), or tiny eight-holed bell caps x 2

Bamboo skewer or medium brass rod, sharpened

Scrap of thin leather

Tacky glue

Superglue

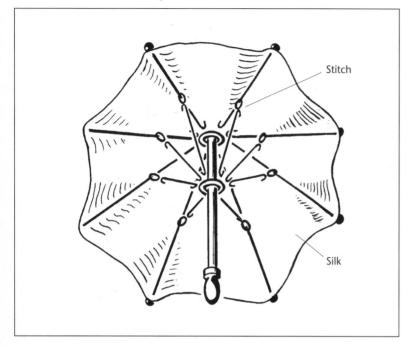

Stitch

Silk

spokes at right angles, then intermediate spokes. Trim away any surplus fabric with manicure scissors.

10 Sew trim to edge of fabric to neaten.

11 Cut a tiny leather circle with a hole punch, pierce the centre and glue onto tip of skewer with tacky glue.

12 Saturate umbrella with spray starch and shape into folds.

13 To open and close umbrella, gently raise and lower the lower jump ring, or bell cap.

14 Any handle can be added to the end of the skewer or rod once it's trimmed to size – about 2½in (64mm). To make a gentleman's wooden umbrella handle, smooth a thin layer of brown Fimo (or Milliput) over the handle only. Harden, paint a wood colour and coat with clear lacquer. Trim handle back so it's clear of the mechanism when the umbrella is shut. Glue a thin strip of brass around the base of the handle.

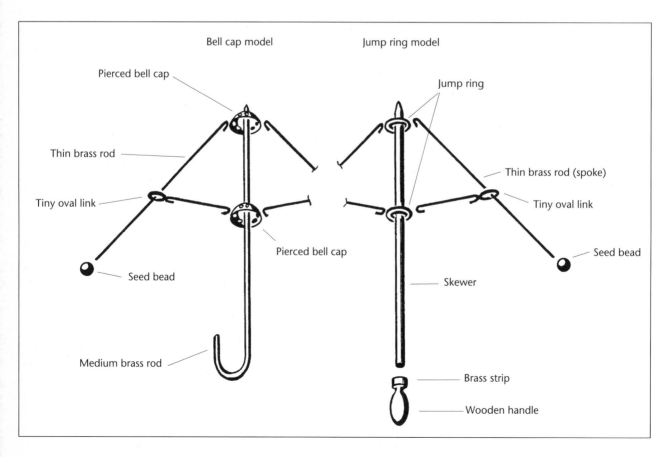

Bell cap model

Jump ring model

Pierced bell cap

Jump ring

Thin brass rod

Thin brass rod (spoke)

Tiny oval link

Tiny oval link

Pierced bell cap

Seed bead

Seed bead

Skewer

Medium brass rod

Brass strip

Wooden handle

CHAPTER SEVEN

Food

Cottage Loaf

There are various recipes for salt dough, which is one of the oldest and cheapest modelling materials. Some people advise adding a drop of antiseptic to discourage mould if damp is likely to be a problem. My oldest cottage loaf, made from just plain flour, salt and water, is nearly 20 years old and still going strong, with no sign of mould.

METHOD

1 Mix salt and flour to a dry soft dough by adding a little water. Knead a little to mix.
2 To make cottage loaf, press a small dough roll onto a larger one. Poke a central hole with a skewer. (Don't make it too perfect, a cottage loaf is rarely finely crafted!)

3 Brush tops of loaves with milk, with a small paintbrush. These areas will brown in the oven.
4 Bake in a conventional oven on a central shelf at 350°F (180°C). Check for colour after 30–35 minutes. Adjust temperature and cooking time according to your oven. Cooking time can be cut down if loaves are hardened in a microwave for a few minutes on the lowest setting, before browning in the oven.
5 When loaves are cool, a little brown pastel can be rubbed on for further colour.
6 Dust with a little talcum powder to look like flour.
7 Once hardened, your loaf can be sliced if required, by placing in a mitre lock and cutting off thin slices with a junior hacksaw.

Materials

1 part salt

1 part plain flour

Water

Drop of antiseptic (optional)

Milk

Talcum powder

Here are suggestions for some other shapes: cut clean slits with a sharp craft knife in the top of a rectangular or round loaf. For a plaited loaf, plait three thin sausages together.

Less refined wholemeal or brown bread was eaten below stairs and in working class households. To make brown bread, mix in a little course ground pepper, or similar, to add colour and texture.

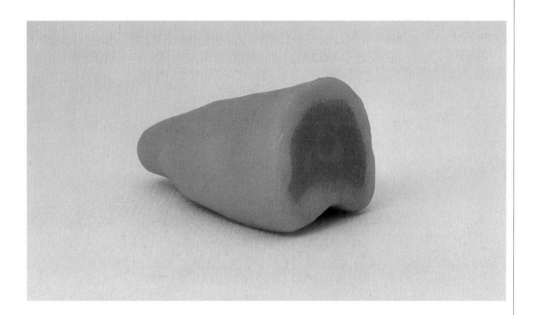

Ham Joint

This tasty joint of ham could be hung in a meat safe. (*See* page 127.)

METHOD

1 Mix transparent Fimo with a little red to make pink. Mix in a scrap of yellow and a speck of black to make ham colour.
2 Mix a scrap of yellow with transparent to make fat colour.
3 Mix transparent with a scrap of red and yellow to make orange, then add a speck of brown to make skin colour.
4 Mix a little fat with ham to marble it slightly – don't over mix. (Keep a little fat and ham back.) Shape into a leg joint. Roll out fat and skin thinly. Wrap fat around joint, followed by skin, blend in any overlap.
5 To make bone, roll a tiny sausage of ham. Flatten a piece of fat and roll around ham sausage. Poke a hole in the end of joint and insert the bone. Poke in a couple of thin strips of fat in the same way.
6 Using a sharp knife, cut off the first slice of ham and discard to reveal a perfect joint. Slice off another, if you like, but don't chop up the whole leg!

7 Shape the joint before cooking. This is the only chance you get to press your fingerprints all over your work, it adds to the texture.

To hang, bend a short piece of thin brass wire to hook through the end of the joint (not shown in illustration).

---

8 Harden in a cool oven 210°F (100°C) for 15 minutes.
9 When cool, glaze end of ham with clear varnish to give it a wet look.

Materials

Fimo: red, white, transparent and yellow

Thin brass wire (not shown in illustration)

Clear varnish

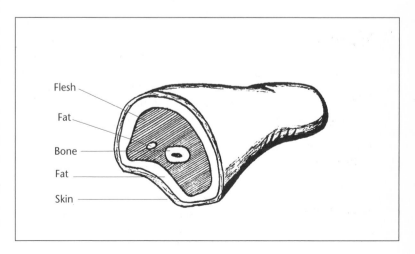

Flesh

Fat

Bone

Fat

Skin

Cakes on Cake Stand

This stand can be used as a centrepiece for a table setting or placed on a side table at high tea.

Materials

Clear plastic buttons
x 2

Clear plastic shank
button

Solid brass rod,
½in (1mm)

Fimo: white, yellow,
brown and red

Nail polish: red

Bathroom sealant:
white

Superglue

METHOD

STAND

1 Drill a ½in (1mm) hole in the centre of all three buttons.
2 Thread the brass rod through all three buttons, placing the shank button at the base with the shank uppermost. Glue rod into shank.
3 Glue the next button a little way up the rod and the last button a little further up.
4 Bend the top of the rod into a looped handle, using thin-nosed pliers. Snip off excess rod.
5 If the button holes are visible, they can be filled with superglue to disguise them.

JAM TARTS

1 Mix a small amount of white Fimo with a little yellow and brown plus a speck of red to make a pastry colour.

2 Roll out the pastry very thinly on greaseproof paper using a piece of thick brass tube, or similar.

I use ⁵⁄₁₆in (8mm) brass tubing as a plain cutter and a ribbed bell cap to give a fluted effect.
---

3 Cut out six circles with cutters. Shape into tarts by gently pushing through a large ¼in (6mm) diameter eyelet with the end of a paintbrush.
4 Place tarts on a baking tray to give them a flat bottom.
5 Roll tiny bits of red Fimo to stand for strawberry pieces. Drop a few into each tart case. Harden in a cooling oven.
6 Once cool, drip one drop of red nail varnish into each tart. Once this dries it congeals to reveal the strawberries, just like real jam tarts.

MERINGUES

1 Fill a small polythene bag with a little white bathroom sealant. Twist bag closed like an icing bag. Cut off the very tip of one corner with nail scissors.
2 Pipe sealant in a tiny circle, pressing into the piping, then quickly remove the icing bag to leave a tail. Practise making a few first. Pipe several onto greaseproof paper and leave to set.
3 Once set, peel paper from meringues. Stick the cakes to the stand with a little Grip Wax.

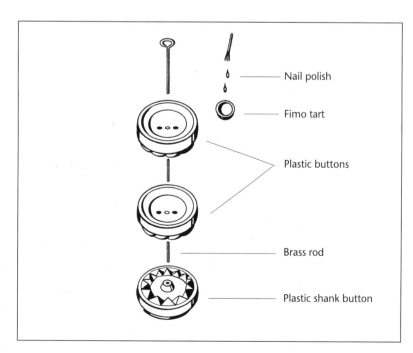

Nail polish

Fimo tart

Plastic buttons

Brass rod

Plastic shank button

String of Garlic

Garlic bulbs were harvested in season, perhaps from the kitchen garden, and stored on a string in a cool dry place, such as the larder, to be used throughout the year.

METHOD

1 Blend a speck of brown Fimo with white to make an off-white. Roll into several pea-sized balls.
2 Thread a Fimo ball onto a darning needle. Shape the top of the ball into a point and press a little to make it less round.
3 Shape clove indents using a cocktail stick. Gently remove garlic bulb from the needle and place base down on a baking tray.
4 Repeat for each bulb, then harden all bulbs in a cool oven for 10 minutes at 250°F (130°C).
5 Brush a little pink acrylic paint onto the base of each bulb once cool.
6 Cut short lengths of raffia. Thread through the holes in the bulbs from the base.

You may need to thin down the raffia to get it through the hole.

---

7 Put a little glue onto the fat end of the bulb, fray the raffia end and press it down onto the bulb bottom. Stick a little more raffia into the hole, fray and trim.

8 Plait three of the garlic strings together, then add remaining strings until they are all plaited in. Plait the bulbs in closely and keep the plait tight.
9 Plait the raffia beyond the last bulb. Fold the plait over, divide the raffia in half and wind one half back the opposite way before tying off.

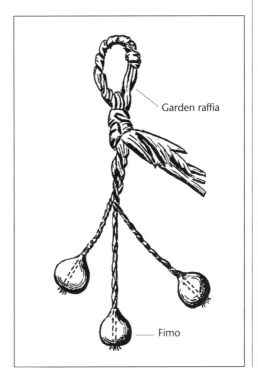

Garden raffia

Fimo

Materials

Fimo: white and brown

Natural garden raffia

Tacky glue

Acrylic paint: pale pink

Materials

Fimo: yellow, red, transparent, blue, white and grey

Blue hairs, e.g. from a jumper or carpet

Talcum powder

Thin brass rod, ½in (1mm)

Thin brass beading wire

Large flat wooden button

Belaying pin (from model shipbuilding suppliers)

Tiny eyelet

Greaseproof paper

Scrap of cellophane

Tacky glue

Acrylic paint: brown

Pastel: mid-brown

Stilton Cheese and Slice

I discovered how to make realistic veined cheese completely by accident. It happened while I was breaking one of my own rules about not working with Fimo while wearing a fluffy jumper. The Fimo happened to be cream, the jumper happened to be blue and a piece of highly convincing veined Stilton was the chance result. Blue carpet fluff is equally effective.

METHOD

CHEESE BOARD AND SLICE

1 Fill thread holes of wooden button with Milliput. Once hardened, sand and paint with wood tones to disguise Milliput.

2 Carefully bend the thin brass rod into the shape shown.

3 Tightly wrap a length of thin beading wire round the short end of the rod and knot securely.

4 Stretch the wire tightly across to the opposite end, wrap around handle and secure. Clip off excess wire.

5 Glue the tiny eyelet onto the handle end of the rod, covering the end of the beading wire to neaten.

6 Glue the belaying pin into the eyelet end.

If the wire is not quite taut enough, gently pull the slice open a little to tighten it.

STILTON

1 Mix a scrap of yellow and a speck of red into white Fimo to give a pale yellow/orange. Mix this in with transparent to give a large

marble-sized ball. Blend well.

2 Pick some blue fluff off something hairy. Try a blanket, jumper or carpet. Blend in just enough to create a veined effect.

3 Blend a speck of blue and grey Fimo together. Press a few specks of this in to look like deeper veins.

4 Shape into a triangle, or a round with a slice cut out.

5 Press the triangle into the cellophane to give both sides a textured edge. Do likewise to the top and bottom.

6 Smooth the remaining side, the rind, into a curve. To colour rind, press on talcum powder and a little brown pastel.

7 Unwrap and place on baking tray. Using a pin, draw a few cracks on both sides and score some crisscross lines on the rind.

8 Harden in a cooling oven for 15 minutes at 210°F (100°C). Before Stilton cools, scrape and nibble (with your finger nail!) a few

bits off the cut sides to resemble crumbly cheese.

9 Once cool, spray the rind with spray mount and press on a little more talc.

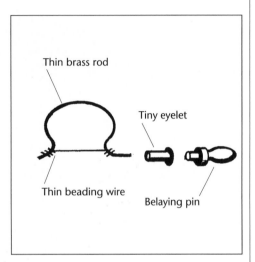

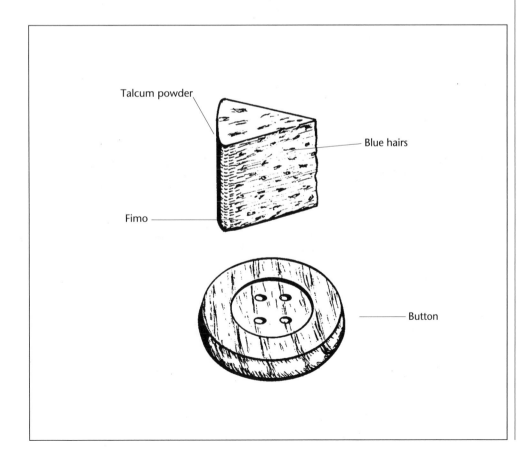

Fried Breakfast

Why not serve up a traditional English breakfast for the whole family in your 1930s house. The mushrooms and tomatoes are made using a glass or pearl-headed dressmakers' pin as a modelling tool.

METHOD

PLATE

1 Fill in buttonholes with Milliput. When hardened, paint or spray plate white.

FRIED EGG

1 Mix a small amount of tacky glue with an equal amount of white acrylic paint. Before it dries, put onto greaseproof paper and swirl into a fried egg shape using a cocktail stick. Leave to dry.

2 When dry, mix yellow and a pinprick of red acrylic paint with tacky glue to make egg yolk yellow. Using a cocktail stick, dot the yolk onto the egg white and leave to dry.

MUSHROOMS

1 Mix a speck of yellow and brown Fimo to make a muddy cream colour. Taking a peppercorn-sized ball, press the pinhead into it to make a well.

2 Mix grey Fimo and a speck of black to make nearly black. Roll a tiny ball and press into a circle. Make radiating cuts round the edge with a craft knife. Gently lift the circle and place inside the mushroom well. Lightly press home with an ordinary pinhead.

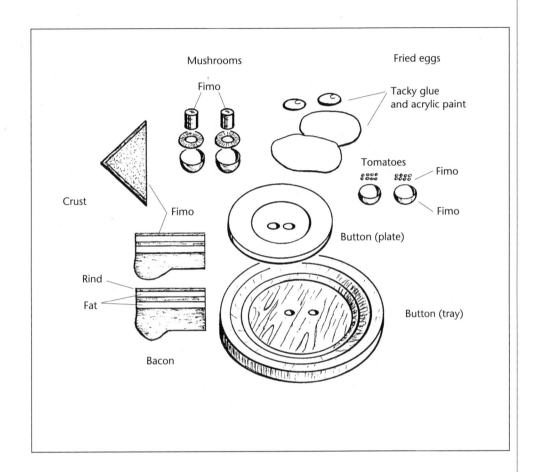

3 Roll a short stalk from the mushroom Fimo and press into the centre.

TOMATOES

1 Mix red Fimo with a speck of yellow. Using a peppercorn-sized ball, make a well in the ball with the pinhead. Fill the well with several tiny specks of orange, for tomato seeds, scraped off a block of Fimo.

FRIED BREAD

1 Mix a speck of yellow and brown Fimo to make a bread colour. Press flat and cut into a small square slice. Edge with a light brown crust made by rolling a thin length of light brown Fimo (blend brown with a speck of white). Press onto slice.

2 Press a piece of coarse sandpaper over the slice to texture it and cut slice in half. Carefully remove from sandpaper with a craft knife.

BACON RASHER

1 Mix red and white Fimo with a speck of black for bacon colour. Add a little white for a marbled effect. Lay a strip of bacon, a thread of white Fimo for fat, followed by a thread of bacon, another thread of white fat and finally a thread of orange Fimo to look like rind. Carefully press together and flatten slightly. Trim the rasher to size with a craft knife. Crinkle it up a little before hardening.

FINISHING

1 Harden all the Fimo food in a cooling oven, 270°F (130°C) for 10 minutes.

2 Arrange food on plate. Mix a pinprick of solvent-based yellow paint with a little clear varnish, or just use clear varnish for fat. Coat the Fimo food with the varnish and drizzle a little onto the plate.

CHAPTER EIGHT

Bedroom
Accessories

Lavender Favour and Potpourri

Potpourri, which translates from French as 'rotten pot', has always had a place in the grand house. In earlier centuries it was carried about to fend off unpleasant street odours. The lavender favour could be placed in an underwear drawer, or hung in the bedroom.

> I use Bio-Preparation salts (sodium stannate crystals) for drying flowers. Cover flowers with a layer of the blue crystals. When crystals turn pink it means they have absorbed moisture. Sieve out flower fragments by pouring crystals through fine tulle, or similar. These fragments can be used for potpourri. Remember to dry out your sodium stannate crystals once they turn pink, since this means they are no longer so absorbent. Place them on the boiler or in the oven at 210°F (100°C) to dry out. When they return to blue they can be re-used. Fuchsia sepals, from the miniature varieties Tinker Belle and Pink Pearls, look just like rose petals when dried.

Lavender Favour

METHOD

1 Gather the stalks together just under the flower heads. (Thin, delicate stalks are best.) Tie a tight double knot round them in the centre of the ribbon. Trim off the flower heads. (When making a full-size favour, the flower heads are left on and encased inside

Materials

Lavender Favour

Lavender stalks x 7

Thin lavender coloured silk ribbon

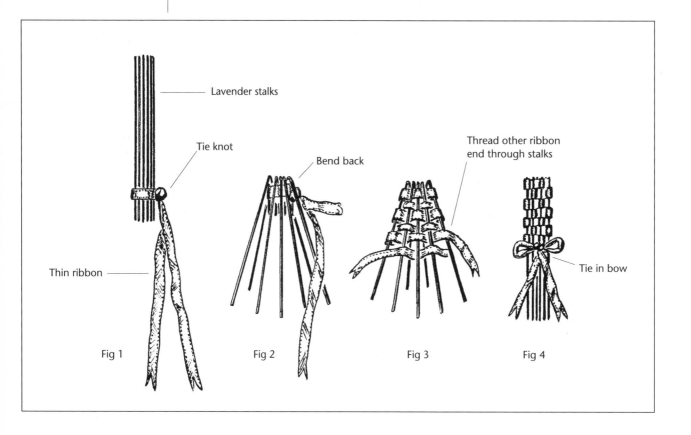

Lavender stalks

Tie knot

Bend back

Thread other ribbon
end through stalks

Thin ribbon

Tie in bow

Fig 1   Fig 2   Fig 3   Fig 4

the favour cage.)

2 Bend all the stalks over like an umbrella to conceal the knot (*see* Fig 2). Thread one of the ribbon ends onto a darning needle. Weave the ribbon in and out of the stalks keeping the other end of the ribbon inside. Weave about four alternating rows.

3 Thread the other ribbon end through the stalks (*see* Fig 3) and tie tightly with the first ribbon end to secure.

4 Wrap the ribbons once around the favour, tie into a double knot and bow (*see* Fig 4).

To tie a tiny bow, begin by tying a regular sized bow, then pull both bow ends until the bow loops are small. Pull the loops to tighten the knot. If it is still too big, repeat. If the loops are pulled out entirely you'll have to start again.

---

5 Trim stalks to size. Leave the favour to dry out.

Materials

Potpourri

Dried flower fragments

Decorative button

Spray mount

Potpourri

METHOD

1 Spray the button with spray mount. Sprinkle on dried petals. Fix container to desired surface in room setting with Grip Wax.

This method ensures the petals stay put if the room setting is rocked. It's a wise precaution to ensure your lovingly arranged room settings are tremor-proof. It's also great fun to watch visitors' faces when they knock into a display and are astounded to see the room shake but nothing fall out of place. This is also useful when dusting. The occasional thorough spring-clean is to be recommended, but in the meantime, if everything is secured down to the last doily and flower, a light wafting breeze from a hair drier will keep things reasonably dust free.

Flask and Cup

The Tudor dressing table generally held a candlestick, a flagon or jug of drink and a drinking vessel.

METHOD

FLASK

1 Glue bead to large bell cap. I also glued a small, thick washer between the bead and bell cap and a larger, thin washer beneath them on one of the flasks as shown.
2 Glue eyelet over opposite thread hole.
3 Glue small bell cap over eyelet.
4 Glue gold bead over bell cap thread hole.

5 Select and bend a suitable section of the earring. I used the shell shape as the handle on one and the lid hinge on the other. Glue to bead.

CUP

1 Glue spacer to bell finding. Glue cone to spacer. I trimmed both findings down a little for a better fit.

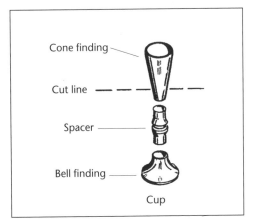

Cone finding

Cut line

Spacer

Bell finding

Cup

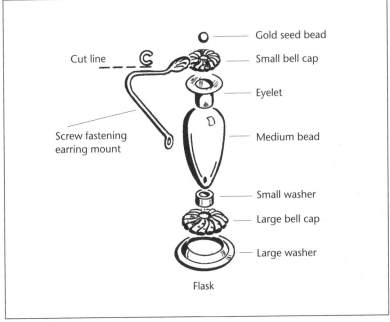

Cut line

Screw fastening earring mount

Gold seed bead

Small bell cap

Eyelet

Medium bead

Small washer

Large bell cap

Large washer

Flask

Cromwellian Stool

Stools with backs (chairs!) didn't make their appearance until the middle of the seventeenth century. Brass nails and wood turning were the only forms of decoration approved by the Puritans. The leather was simply stretched and nailed over the frame, with nothing so luxurious as stuffing yet.

Of course, Tudor furniture would have been much lighter when it was first made than as we see it today. However, I like to stain mine dark – but I don't recommend Jacobean oak wood stain as it's an unnatural blue black shade. Don't apply varnish to Tudor furniture. Apply wax furniture polish, or oil, and buff to produce a patina of wear over time.

The wood sticks are toffee-apple sticks. These are sold in packs near the cocktail sticks. I like them for old furniture because they are delightfully roughly hewn.

METHOD

PREPARATION
1 Stain all the wood dark.

LEGS
1 Sand down a straight skewer so the wood beads fit on snugly. Thread five round beads, then one square, then another round one onto the skewer. Make four such legs.
2 Drill a tiny hole on two adjacent sides of all the square beads (*see* illustration).

STRETCHER
1 Thread five round beads onto a skewer, and whittle ends to fit holes in square beads on legs. Make two such stretchers.
2 Apply wood glue to joins and holes and fit stretchers in between legs, one on either side, ensuring skewers fit into holes.

Materials

Small round wooden beads x 30 (mine are ³⁄₁₆in (5mm))

Small square or rectangular beads x 4

Wood sticks (toffee-apple sticks)

Thin leather (distressed is good)

Bamboo skewers

Wood glue

Fine marker pen: gold

3 Cut two more plain stretchers from toffee-apple sticks and drill a tiny hole in each end.

4 Pare off four tiny pegs of skewer. Glue into stretcher holes and remaining holes in square beads on leg. Repeat for other side.

5 Carefully fit an elastic band around the frame to ensure it dries squarely. Leave to dry for several hours (wood glue takes longer to dry than tacky glue).

SEAT

1 Cut two lengths of toffee-apple stick to fit across opposite sides of stool top. Drill small holes at both ends of each, to fit tops of skewers in legs. Trim skewers to length and glue into holes.

2 Cut two lengths of toffee-apple sticks to fit two remaining opposite sides. Glue into place with tacky glue (wood glue is not so effective on flat joints). Secure with a second elastic band and leave to dry.

3 Fit two more struts cut from toffee-apple sticks across top and glue in place.

UPHOLSTERY

1 Smear top of stool with tacky glue and stretch distressed leather over seat. Secure with an elastic band until dry. Trim away excess leather.

2 Mark gold dots around the edge of seat with a fine gold marker pen, to look like brass nails.

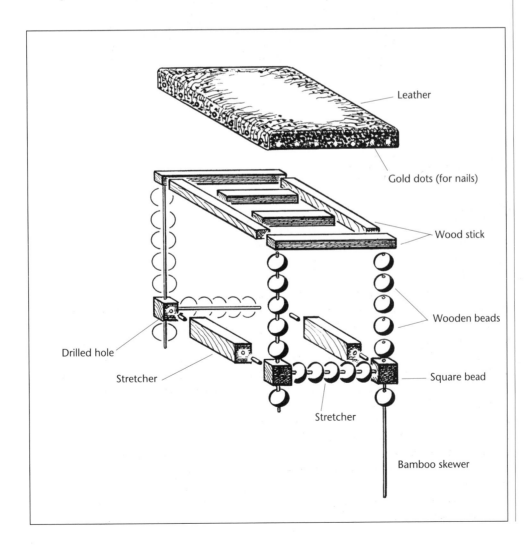

Materials

Superfine Milliput

Tiny floral picture clippings (not shown in illustration)

Medium brass wire, ½in (1mm)

White seed beads x 3

Gold seed beads x 2

Acrylic paint: white

Clear varnish

Thin marker pen: gold

Transfer emulsion

Superglue

Chamber Pot and Slop Bucket

The used chamber pot was placed next to the bucket on the lower shelf of the washstand to be emptied by the maid. No wonder many servants opted for shop or factory work as soon as it became available.

METHOD

SLOP BUCKET

1 Roll a marble-sized ball of Milliput and place on a smooth working surface. Poke a central hole into it with a wooden skewer (or similar) and enlarge with an orange stick until the hollow is large enough to accommodate a modelling tool with a ball-end (you can improvise one by fixing a bead to the skewer).

Hollow it out to make a rudimentary pot.

2 Draw pot up and out slightly with your fingertips, thinning sides as you go. Once sides are regular, set aside to harden for about 15 minutes.

3 Trim top evenly with manicure scissors and poke a small hole through both sides to take handle, using a darning needle. Smooth away any fingerprints. Leave to harden.

4 Thread three white seed beads onto brass wire. Bend one end into a right angle with pliers. Curve wire, measure against bucket and snip to size. Bend a right angle into other end. Shape handle evenly with pliers before stretching it to fit into the holes on bucket.

5 Glue a gold seed bead onto each end of handle, inside bucket, to fix in place.

6 Apply a dot of superglue to seed beads to keep them in place at top of handle.

CHAMBER POT

1 Roll a pea-sized ball of Milliput and flatten to form a thin base the size of a small coin. Set aside to harden.

2 Repeat step 1 of bucket method, above.

3 Work ball-shaped modelling tool inside pot so that it bulges out a little. Pull a small lip around edge of pot. Set aside to harden for about 15 minutes.

4 Trim lip using manicure scissors. Carefully press pot onto base and set aside to harden.

5 Roll a thin length of Milliput. Holding pot upside down, press one end of handle onto pot a little way up from lip so that handle hangs down. Turn pot upright and allow handle to fall into a curve. Press other end of handle to base of pot and pinch off excess. I pinched a tip to my handle to match my water jug. Set aside to harden.

DECORATION

1 Use white acrylic paint to wash over bucket and pot.

2 Once dry, stick on tiny transfers made from transfer emulsion (*see* page 7).

3 Draw round the rims with a gold marker pen and leave to dry for 24 hours.

4 Paint clear varnish over bucket, handle grip and chamber pot to give a porcelain effect.

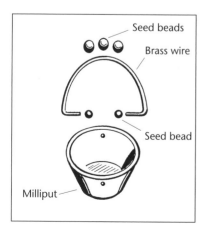

Seed beads

Brass wire

Seed bead

Milliput

Milliput pot and handle

Milliput base

Tudor Four-Poster Bed

My original intention was to make a very plain sixteenth century bed and reflect the wealth of the prosperous owners in richly decorated drapes. However, with the addition of a few beads and mouldings, I found an ornate bed quite straightforward to put together. There's practically no woodwork. Tudor furniture wasn't precision made like modern furniture: this suits me, I hate too many exacting measurements.

The bedstead proper should be low and free standing, attached to the framework at the head only. Try to find pieces of suitably old and weathered wood. I used some which came from an old wardrobe of my Grandmother's. Any bare wood strips will do as they will all be stained a uniform colour.

> Tudor black oak wood stain sounds tempting but don't be surprised if it comes up very dark navy blue. Black stain or dye is bound to be concentrated navy or purple since a true black cannot be synthesized. I used two coats of Jacobean dark oak.

Materials

Wood strip, ¾ x ⅛in
(19 x 3.0mm)

Cornice moulding
lengths x 2

Decorative beading
lengths x 2

Thin wood sheet

Thin wood sheet, ¹⁄₁₆
x 4in (1.5 x 102mm)

Wood strip, ³⁄₁₆ x ½in
(4.5 x 12.5mm)

Thin wood strip, ¹⁄₁₆ x
¼in (1.5 x 6.5mm)

Filigree decorations x 3

Large and small
wooden bead pairs,
preferably carved or
decorated

Decorative wooden
beads x 2

Straight skewers x 2

Large square wood
post, approx. ⅝in
(16mm)

Small square wood
post, ¼in (6.5mm)

Banister spindles x 2

Wood strip, ⅛ x ½in
(3.0 x 12.5mm)

Continued...

Fig 8.1 Decorative beads and wood strip

METHOD

PREPARATION

1 Stain all wood parts before gluing. Any glue will repel stain and give the bed an uneven, patchy finish.

CANOPY

1 From ¾ x ⅛in (19 x 3.0mm) wood strip, cut two lengths of 4¾in (121mm) and two lengths of 6in (152mm). Mitre ends and glue to form a rectangle. Butt into a jig until dry.

2 Cut four lengths of cornice moulding to fit outside edges of canopy. Mitre edges of cornice and glue to canopy.

3 Cut lengths of decorative beading to fit below cornice. Mitre edges and glue in place. Set aside to dry.

4 Cut a piece of thin wood sheet to fit into canopy roof.

> **Since I didn't have any wood sheet large enough, I used a section of ply from a wooden vegetable crate. This was easily cut to size using power scissors.**

HEADBOARD

1 From ¹⁄₁₆ x 4in (1.5 x 102mm) wood sheet, cut a 5½in (140mm) length. Glue this inside one of the shorter sides of the canopy, level with the top edge, as a backing for the headboard.

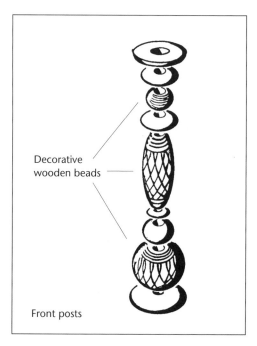

Decorative
wooden beads

Front posts

2 From ³⁄₁₆ x ½in (4.5 x 12.5mm) wood strip, cut two lengths of 6½in (165mm). Glue one each side of canopy, on top of sheet, at back inside corners, to make the back legs.

3 From ¹⁄₁₆ x ¼in (1.5 x 6.5mm) wood strip, cut and glue strips to fit down and across headboard, to resemble panelling.

4 Paint filigree decorations with wood colour and glue into panels.

FRONT POSTS

1 Thread a selection of wooden beads onto straight skewers to resemble two carved posts. The beads may need sanding to give matching heights.

2 Cut two lengths from the large square post to make up the height of the post to 6½in (165mm) (the height of headboard).

3 Drill a straight central hole in each post (so the skewer sits square). Remove beads from skewers and glue skewers into holes.

4 Fill bead holes with wood filler, e.g. Cascamite. Before this hardens, re-thread beads onto skewers, positioning squarely on top of each other. Set posts aside to harden.

5 From small square post cut two ½in (12.5mm) lengths. Drill a hole centrally through each. Thread the top of each skewer into each hole. Glue these inside the front corners of the canopy. Press decorative beads onto tops of skewers and snip off excess skewer when posts are level.

6 Use an offcut of cornice moulding to make a mitred edge for three sides of each front post. Glue in place.

7 Sand banister spindles flat on one side and glue to front of posts.

BEDSTEAD

1 From ⅛ x ½in (3.5mm x 12.5mm) wood strip, cut two 5in (127mm) lengths for side struts. Join together with Blu-Tack and drill seven roughly spaced holes to take the twine.

2 From ⅛ x ½in (3.5 x 12.5mm) wood strip, cut a 3⅞in (10cm) length for front bedstead strut.

3 From small square post, cut two 1½in (38mm) lengths. Cut a recess into two adjacent sides of these posts to fit side and front struts of bedstead, using a sharp craft knife.

4 Glue above three struts in place with Araldite for a strong bond.

5 From ⅛ x ½in (3.5 x 12.5mm) wood strip, cut a 4in (102mm) length for back bedstead strut. Glue between side bedstead struts and onto back posts with Araldite.

6 Once dry, thread twine through holes in side struts of bedstead, to support mattress. Tie a double knot at each end to secure.

FINISHING

1 Fill any gaps in the frame with wood filler, smooth off and sand lightly when hardened.

2 Sand any rough areas with fine sandpaper.

3 Apply a coat of Danish oil, followed by a coat of wax furniture polish, using a soft toothbrush. Rub in well and buff to a sheen with a soft cloth.

Brown twine, e.g. thick crochet cotton dyed with tea

Wood filler, e.g. Cascamite

Wood glue

Araldite

Dark oak wood stain

Acrylic paint: various browns

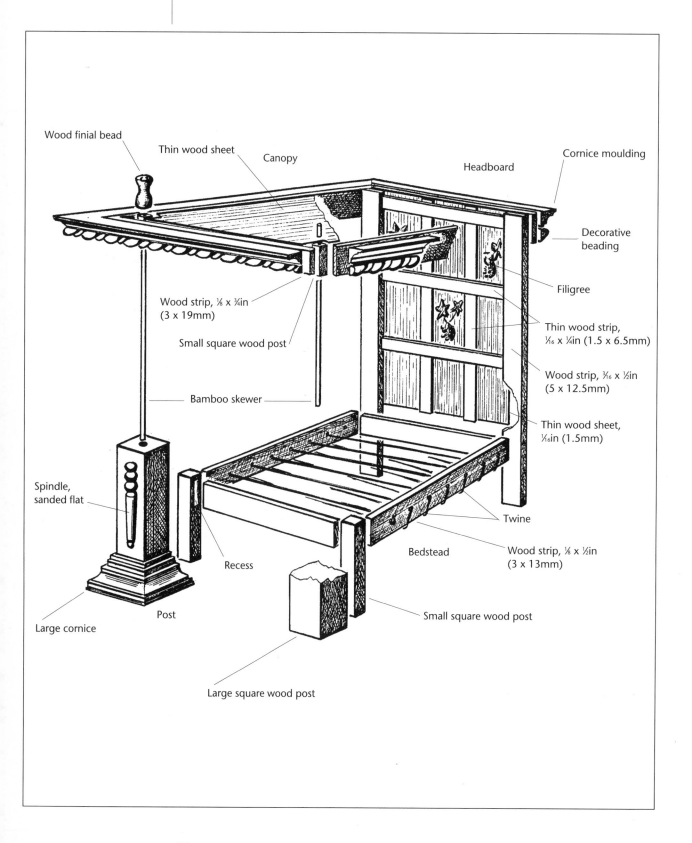

Wood finial bead

Thin wood sheet

Canopy

Headboard

Cornice moulding

Decorative beading

Filigree

Wood strip, ⅛ x ¾in (3 x 19mm)

Small square wood post

Thin wood strip, ¹⁄₁₆ x ¼in (1.5 x 6.5mm)

Wood strip, ³⁄₁₆ x ½in (5 x 12.5mm)

Bamboo skewer

Thin wood sheet, ¹⁄₁₆in (1.5mm)

Spindle, sanded flat

Twine

Bedstead

Wood strip, ⅛ x ½in (3 x 13mm)

Recess

Post

Small square wood post

Large cornice

Large square wood post

CHAPTER NINE

Nursery
Accessories

Materials

Wood strip, ¹⁄₁₆ x ⅛in
(1.5 x 3mm)

Thin wood veneer
strip

Solid brass rod,
¹⁄₃₂in (1mm)

Gold seed beads

Wood glue

Superglue

Shoe polish: black

Abacus

Often seen in the nursery, the abacus has been around since ancient times. It could be described as the forerunner of the calculator – in fact it is still used in some parts of the world.

If an abacus had a horizontal division it was known as a heaven and earth abacus. The lower beads were units of one and the upper were units of five.

METHOD

FRAME

1 Cut two 1in (25.5mm) lengths and two ¹¹⁄₁₆in (17.5mm) lengths of wood strip.
2 Mitre the ends so that the four pieces make a rectangular frame. Don't glue together yet.
3 Cut a length of thin wood veneer to the same length as the long strips and sandwich it between long strips with Blu-Tack. Lightly sand edges.

To avoid abrading fingers when sanding small items, wrap parcel tape around fingertips.

---

4 Mark seven points in pencil, ⅛in (3mm) apart, along the three sandwiched lengths.
5 Drill a tiny hole, ¹⁄₃₂in (1mm), through each point. Remove Blu-Tack, but keep matching drill holes lined up. Lightly sand down holes.

To remove Blu-Tack residue from wood grain rub a ball of Blu-Tack over area. This will pull any stubborn bits out that may spoil the finish.

---

6 Glue the frame together using wood glue. Line up and glue in the thin wood veneer divider. (Use a brass rod to line holes up.) Place frame in a jig to keep straight whilst it dries. (I use the corner of a rectangular tray as a jig.)

BEADS

1 Snip seven brass rods to about 1in (25.5mm) long. Thread brass rods through lower holes, thread five seed beads onto each rod, thread rod through thin wood veneer divider, thread on two more seed beads and thread through top hole.
2 Apply a dot of superglue into each bottom hole to secure rod. Snip top of rods close to frame with wire cutters. Secure tops of rods with superglue. Lightly sand down top, bottom and corners.

DISTRESSING

1 Polish abacus with a dot of black shoe polish, using a toothbrush.

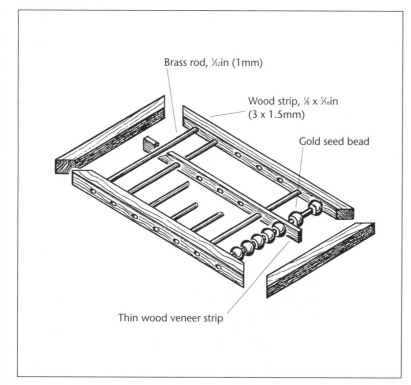

Brass rod, ¹⁄₃₂in (1mm)

Wood strip, ⅛ x ¹⁄₁₆in
(3 x 1.5mm)

Gold seed bead

Thin wood veneer strip

Materials

Chip of slate

Chip of chalk

Thin miniature picture frame moulding, with rebate

Tacky glue

Writing Slate

Where feasible I prefer using authentic materials to make my miniatures – tiny fragments of old slate can often be found in old churchyards. Some dolls' house suppliers stock dolls' house roofing slate.

METHOD

SLATE

1 Clip down the slate to a small rectangle, with power scissors (mine measures $^{11}/_{16}$ x ¾in (17.5 x 19mm)). Sand both sides smooth with fine sandpaper and square off edges.
2 Cut two lengths of moulding for the top and bottom of the slate, and two for the sides. (The slate will fit into the rebate exactly like a picture does.)
3 Mitre the edges and glue together to form a frame. Repeat steps 2 and 3 for the back of the slate.
4 Fit the slate between the two frames and glue together. You may need to sand the slate a little for a good fit.
5 Round off the frame edges and sand the frame down flatter so it doesn't look too much like a picture frame.

CHALK AND CLOTH

1 Pare off a small piece of chalk from a full-size piece. Trim to shape roughly with a craft knife.

2 Roll the chalk stick gently (so it doesn't snap) back and forth on an emery board to smooth it.
3 Sand one end level and the other to a slant.
4 Cut up a snippet of duster for the cloth.

You could try knitting a cloth like I did. I knitted garter stitch on T-pins, using darning wool. The stitches don't have to be perfect. Old cards of darning wool can often be unearthed in charity shops.

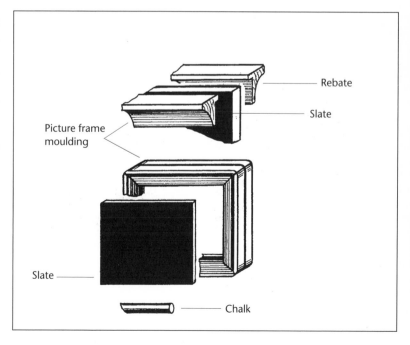

Picture frame moulding

Rebate

Slate

Slate

Chalk

Silver Whistle Rattle

These rattles, with a whistle at the top, bells on the sides and a coral teething stick on the bottom, were enough to keep any Victorian baby amused. The coral had dual purpose – it was thought to ward off witchcraft. Choose nickel findings for a silver-look finish or use gilt findings which can be silver-plated before assembly.

Materials

Small torpedo clasp, hole half

Small pierced bell cap

Small ribbed hogans (diamond-shaped findings) x 4

Ribbed finding, fluted at both ends

Tiny tulip bell cap

Long coral bead: white, pink or red

Dressmakers' pin

Thin nickel beading wire

Araldite

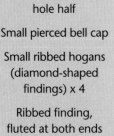

METHOD

HANDLE (TEETHING STICK)
1 Cut one end off the fluted finding. Sand cut end.
2 Glue coral bead into tulip bell cap.
3 Glue bead and bell cap to trimmed end of fluted finding with the aid of the pin, stuck through the thread holes, covered in glue.

BELLS
1 Bend a length of wire in half, leaving a loop at the bend.
2 Thread a hogan finding onto the two ends of the wire. Make sure it is stopped by the loop and doesn't fall off.
3 Thread the wire ends through the holes in one side of the pierced bell cap. Twist the wires inside to hold the bell in place. (Don't secure too tightly, the bell should rattle.) Attach three more bells to the pierced bell cap.
4 Glue the pierced bell cap with four attached bells to the handle section.

WHISTLE
1 Glue the torpedo clasp half to the top of the pierced bell cap to stand for the whistle.
2 Paint a small black square onto the top to look like an air hole.

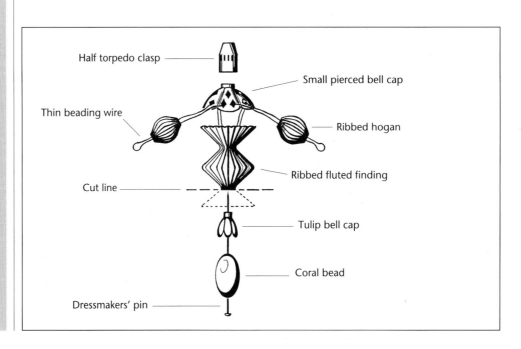

Half torpedo clasp

Thin beading wire

Cut line

Dressmakers' pin

Small pierced bell cap

Ribbed hogan

Ribbed fluted finding

Tulip bell cap

Coral bead

Cuckoo Clock

The original cuckoo clocks were fashioned in the Black Forest in Germany from the 1850s until the 1940s. The hands on this clock are adjustable, complying with a rather strict direction I once read that all the clocks in a dolls' house should tell the same time. The filigrees are from egg crafting suppliers.

METHOD

CLOCK BODY

1 Sand any old varnish off the building block and stain oak.
2 Prime and paint in a wood tone, the decorative finding, left and right birds, oak leaves and round, pierced filigree (dial). Set aside the third oak leaf.
3 Once dial and decorations are dry, glue in place on block as shown.
4 Cut two lengths of medium wood strip to make a roof. Mitre the two edges to fit together at the apex. Glue to top of clock body, either side of decorative finding.

PENDULUM

1 Glue the third oak leaf to the end of a thin wood strip and cut to length (about height of block again) to make a pendulum.
2 Fix a small jump ring to the opposite end. Attach this to the tiny screw-eye.
3 Drill a deep hole in base of clock. Screw screw-eye into the hole so that pendulum swings freely.

WEIGHTS

1 Cut down and carefully press and glue an eye pin into the top of each tiny cone.
2 Attach an eye pin to each end of the chain with jump rings.
3 Glue the chain to the back of the clock so that the cones hang at different heights.

The smallest cones I've managed to find aren't true cones at all. They are the female catkin of the common Alder, often found near water. Its true cones are also fairly small and useful for Christmas decorations.

DIAL

1 Paint the two eye pins white: a white spray primer gives an even finish.
2 Press a tiny brass nail into the centre of the block to make a hole.
3 Paint a tiny dash of white on the pierced dial for each hour.
4 Trim down and thread the two painted eye pins onto the tiny brass nail. Thread nail into the dial centre and push into the clock body.

Materials

Small wooden building block

Thin wood strip

Medium wood strip

Gilt birds (left and right)

Gilt leaves x 3 (preferably oak)

Decorative filigree finding

Belaying pin

Thin brass wire

Round pierced filigree (for dial)

Tiny dried alder cones, or similar, x 8

Gilt trace chain

Tiny eye pins x 2

Tiny screw-eye

Tiny brass nail

Medium jump rings x 3

Acrylic paint: shades of brown

Spray primer: white

Araldite

French polish

Wood stain: dark or medium oak

Fine felt-tipped pen: black

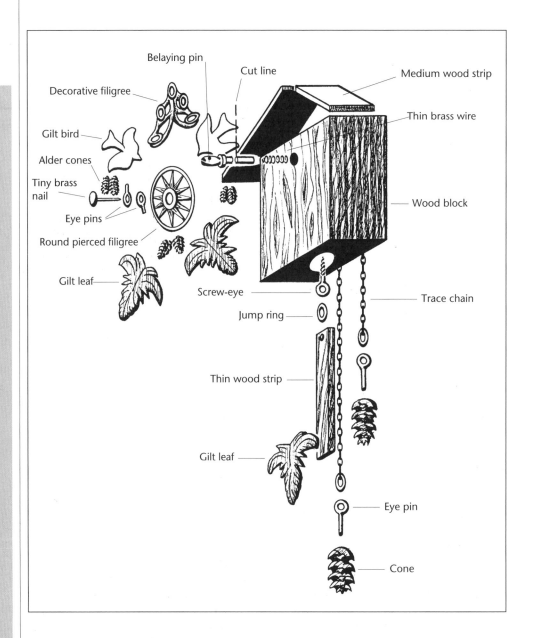

FINISH

1 Coat pendulum, body, body trim, dial and cones with French polish to give a uniform appearance of polished wood.

CUCKOO

1 Drill a small hole, ³⁄₃₂in (2.4mm), through block, centred in the upper section of the clock.

2 Sand the rounded end of the belaying pin to roughly resemble a bird's head. Dot on two eyes with felt pen. (Upon the insistence of my husband, I had to glue a tiny Milliput beak to my bird and paint it yellow.)

3 Snip off the pointed end of the belaying pin and discard. Make a coiled spring to fit the end of the pin by wrapping thin brass wire round a cocktail stick. Glue the bird into this coil.

4 Twist the coil into the hole. Snip off excess coil at the back.

Wax Doll

This nineteenth century Pierotti-style doll (Pierotti was an English doll manufacturer) is more straightforward to make than she first appears. The original has a fabric body (stuffed with horsehair). Wax was poured into a sculpted mould to make the head and limbs.

Transparent Fimo is an excellent medium for making a doll with limbs that look like poured wax. The original measured 24in (61cm); I scaled my miniature version down to just 1½in (about 38mm). Any bigger and dolls can become confused with small nursery occupants. Once you have the basic doll the clothing can be as simple or as intricate as you like.

Gimp, or lampshade trim, is too bulky to be of much use in the dolls' house. When pulled apart, however, it makes enchanting dolls' ringlets.

METHOD

ARMS, LEGS AND HEAD

1 Blend scraps of yellow and red Fimo to make orange. Blend a scrap of the orange with transparent to make tints varying from pink to peach.

2 Roll a length of Fimo wax about ³⁄₃₂in (2.5mm) wide for arms. At one end roll a waist for the wrist. Flatten beyond the wrist to make the hand. Trim excess away with a craft knife. Cut a rough thumb shape and a few indents for fingers – don't try to make individual fingers. The end result should resemble a tiny mitten. Make two arms.

3 Roll a thin length of Fimo ⅛in (3mm) wide. Shape into a simple foot at one end. Make two legs.

4 You can model the head yourself, but since a mould is used for the original, the following method is more appropriate. Take a Milliput cast of a small face from a plastic doll (I used

Materials

Fimo: transparent, yellow and red

Scrap of cotton fabric

Scrap of gimp (lampshade trim)

Blue seed beads

Cotton wool

Scrap of silk for clothes (not shown in illustration)

Scrap of trimmings for clothes (not shown in illustration)

Tacky glue

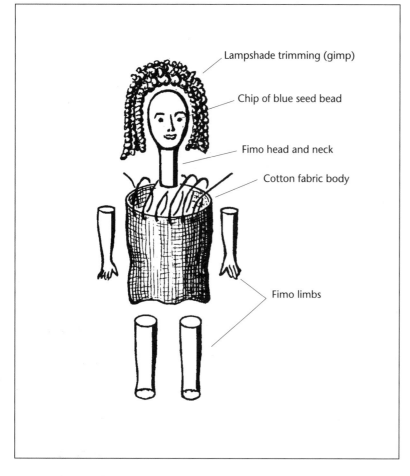

Lampshade trimming (gimp)

Chip of blue seed bead

Fimo head and neck

Cotton fabric body

Fimo limbs

Pick up chip with a pinhead dipped in tacky glue. There is no need to glue chip in.

7 Harden all body parts in a cooling oven, 100°C (210°F), for 10 minutes. When cool refine shape of arms and back of head with an emery board.

WIG
1 Unravelled gimp results in either kinked curls or dense coils. Carefully pull the thread from the centre of a coil to reveal a miniscule ringlet.
2 Thread a length of unravelled gimp onto a thin needle and sew a centre parting back and forth down the middle of five coiled ringlets, leaving some loops at one end to make a fringe.
3 Smear head thinly with tacky glue and press wig in place.

BODY AND CLOTHES
1 Sew a cotton sack about 7⁄16 x 5⁄8in (11.2 x 16mm). Turn right side out. Stuff lightly with cotton wool. Glue neck of doll into opening and sew up shoulders.
2 Fold and wrap a scrap of silk around one arm, tucking in raw edges. Stitch to secure. Trim with lace at the wrist. Repeat for other arm. Set aside.
3 Make a rudimentary pair of bloomers with a scrap of lace. Stick the legs into the bloomers with tacky glue.
4 Sew another scrap of lace to bloomers for a petticoat. Gather tops of bloomers and petticoat and sew to bottom of body pad.
5 Wrap a scrap of gathered silk around body, tucking in raw edges. Stitch at the back and shoulders to secure. Trim neck of dress with thin ribbon or lace.
6 Sew arms to body, keeping stitching hidden.
7 Tie thin ribbon around body to make a waist. Trim dress with lace and ribbon.
8 Make a simple bonnet with a snippet of plaited straw or embroidery canvas. Trim with ribbon or lace. Glue onto back of head.

a cake decoration cherub) by pressing the ball onto the face. Prise the mould off once hardened.
5 Roll a cone shape in Fimo wax and push into the mould aiming the point at the nose. Press in the rest of the Fimo leaving a stalk for the neck. Leave to cool in the fridge for five minutes then gently ease head away from mould.

In my experience, it is worth making a few casts and choosing the best.

6 Put a few blue seed beads into a polythene bag and crush with a hammer or in a vice. Indent eyes in face with a pinhead. Select two suitable chips, press gently into holes.

Victorian Swinging Cradle

The full-size original is mahogany and comparatively larger. I modified the size since dolls' house nurseries tend to be small rooms. My cradle is stained oak.

METHOD

CRADLE

1 Make up one rectangular side panel with an extended strut for the hood support using two 2¹³⁄₁₆in (71.5mm), one 1⁵⁄₁₆in (33.5mm) and one 2in (51mm) lengths. Glue a 1¹⁄₁₆in (27mm) length as a strut in the centre.

2 Repeat for second side panel.

3 Join above two side panels with the four 1³⁄₁₆in (30mm) lengths to make a rectangular box. Set aside to dry.

HOOD

1 Glue the two ¹¹⁄₁₆in (17.5mm) hood supports to the cradle about ¹¹⁄₁₆in (17.5mm) from the back hood supports.

2 Make up two pointed arches with the four 1in (25.5mm) hood pieces. Mitre both ends to fit hood supports. Glue arches to hood supports.

BASE AND SIDES

1 Cut the lolly stick into planks and glue along base of cradle, evenly spaced.

2 Stain embroidery canvas to match wood, then cut sections to fit inside the cradle, behind wood frame. Glue to inside of cradle.

3 Lightly sand and stain all wood parts. Lightly sand any rough edges.

STAND

1 Drill two level ½in (1mm) holes in the top of the newel posts. Press a brass nail halfway into each hole.

2 Drill two more holes, one below the other, at the other end of each newel post, large enough to take end of banister spindle.

3 Cut two lengths, 1⁹⁄₁₆in (40mm) from the thick wood strip, and glue centrally to base of newel posts using Araldite.

4 Cut down the four banister spindles, to slightly longer than cradle length. Drill holes in cut down ends and glue ends together with a short section of cocktail stick acting as a peg (*see* illustration, over page).

5 Glue spindles above the two banister struts into the newel post holes, as shown.

6 Drill two ½in (1mm) holes in each end of the top of the cradle frame, as shown. Push a brass nail into each hole.

7 Tie twine around one nail. Allowing the cradle

Materials

Thin square wood strip, ⅛in (3mm)

Embroidery canvas

Tiny nails x 6

Thin twine

Lolly stick

Newel posts x 2

Banister spindles, square x 4

Thick wood strip, ⅜in (9.5mm)

Cocktail stick

Thin packing foam

Thin card

Silk

Tacky glue

Woodstain: oak

French polish

to hang level, hook twine over newel post nail and tie onto other nail. Repeat for other end.

8 Finish wood parts with a few coats of French polish.

LINING

1 Cut strips of card to line hood, sides and base.

2 Glue a thin foam layer to the card with small dots of tacky glue.

3 Cover with silk, secured to back with a little tacky glue.

4 Neaten the back view as it may be partially visible through canvas sides.

5 Press covered cards into position in cradle. If necessary they can be secured with a little Grip Wax.

CURTAINS

1 Hem two sides of a small square of silk along top edge. Glue this edge to the wrong side of the covered card strip of the hood, so the bottom of the curtain hangs straight across. Tie curtain back with cotton thread. Make two curtains.

Cutting List

Cradle, from ⅛in (3mm) thin, square wood strip:
2¹³⁄₁₆in (71.5mm) x 4

1⅝in (33.5mm) x 2
1¹⁄₁₆in (27mm) x 2
2in (51mm) x 2
1³⁄₁₆in (30mm) x 4

Hood, from ⅛in (3mm) thin, square wood strip:
¹¹⁄₁₆in (17.5mm) x 2
1in (25.5mm) x 4

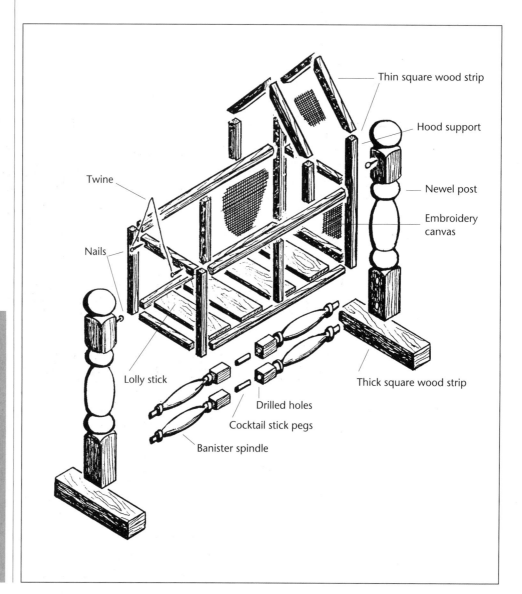

Thin square wood strip

Hood support

Newel post

Embroidery canvas

Twine

Nails

Lolly stick

Thick square wood strip

Drilled holes

Cocktail stick pegs

Banister spindle

Sitting Room
Accessories

Materials

Bronze Statues

Bronze statues of horses or dogs found favour with Georgian collectors. Victorians liked Gothic maidens and the 'animelier style' of casting (a French term meaning 'looking animated'). During the 1920s and 1930s graceful feminine figurines were in vogue.

These bronze statues started life as plastic farmyard horses, cake decorations and cast alloy figures from War games suppliers. The bather needed a touch of fat reduction on her thighs with a craft knife before passing the audition. I painted over her original 1950s bathing costume to give her a more flowing outfit.

METHOD

1 Tidy figure with a craft knife, removing any unsightly lumps or bumps.

Be sure to use a new blade on your craft knife – a blunt one snags plastic.

---

2 Spray with white primer.
3 When dry, paint with two thin coats of bronze. For 1920s style figurines paint flesh ivory and clothing (usually minimal) bronze.
4 Glue to suitable button, over thread holes.
5 For a 1920s and 1930s onyx-style base, streak yellow and white Fimo together with a speck of green. Dot in bits of black. Don't overblend.
6 Shape into a rough block. Cut around block with a craft knife to give a carved effect.
7 Pare base of figurine down to fit into centre of onyx block, but remove during baking. Bake onyx base in cooling oven 210°F (100°C). Glue figurine to base when cool.
8 Mix a very dilute green/blue acrylic wash to use as a patina (discolouration of age). Brush into folds and corners of figure. Smear with your finger as you work.
9 Once dry, spray with clear lacquer to give a metallic gleam.

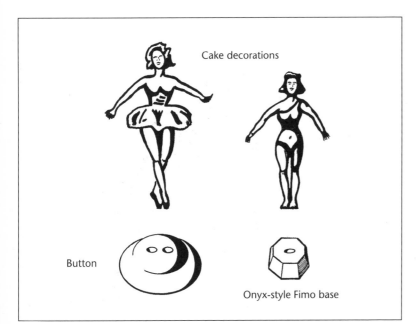

Cake decorations

Button

Onyx-style Fimo base

Trailing Plant

It is possible to buy thin brass cut-out ivy plants which have to be made up and painted. I decided I would save myself the painting by using real ivy. Spring is the best time to collect the tiniest leaves. Pick all your leaves to include the stem.

The stands shown here are simply cotton reels mounted onto buttons. I used gold spray paint to colour one, and alternate coats of black and white on the other to resemble marble.

Keep a small, airtight container handy to collect suitable specimens for drying. (I use a 35mm film capsule.) Fill the container with drying medium, e.g. sodium stannate, so you can pop any floral finds straight in.

Materials

Tiny dried ivy leaves

Drying medium, e.g. sodium stannate

Thin green florists' wire

Tiny lid for pot, e.g. lipstick lid

Blu-Tack

Tea leaves

Tacky glue

METHOD

1 Place the ivy leaves in the drying medium and leave until completely dried out – about a week.

Leaves can be dried in a microwave if you need instant results, but timing needs to be precise. Too long and they will desiccate, too high and the crystals will burn. Use only the lowest power setting for about 10 minutes, then leave undisturbed to cool for another 10 minutes.

2 Fill the pot with Blu-Tack and press tea leaves over the surface to stand for soil.

Fasten the pot to a cotton reel with Blu-Tack. This way the plant will be easier to handle.

3 Wiggle the florists' wire into several stem shapes and smear on a thin coating of tacky glue. This will help the leaf stalks stick.

4 Bend stems at the top and stick into Blu-Tack. Stick a few shorter lengths of wire in to represent new growth.

5 Pick up a small leaf using tweezers and dip the stem in a small puddle of tacky glue. Press gently onto end of wire stem. Arrange in place with a T-pin.

6 Glue leaves, alternating left and right, to the top of the stem.

7 Once all the stems are covered, press a few leaf stalks into the centre of the pot. Leave to dry completely.

8 Gloss can be added to the leaves with a coat of water-based varnish or transfer emulsion. Solvent-based varnish tends to peel off.

9 Place in position and gently trail the stems with tweezers.

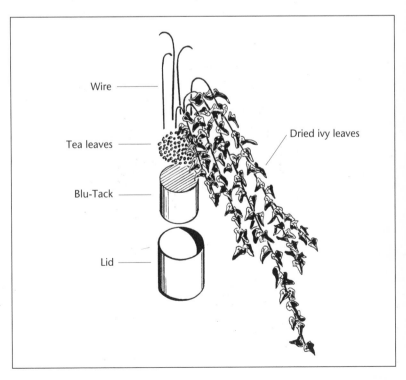

Wire

Tea leaves

Blu-Tack

Lid

Dried ivy leaves

2 Mix equal parts of white and transparent Fimo with a scrap of red to make pink. Flatten a length of Fimo until paper thin. Tear a little off and roll up to make a tiny bud. Try to roll so the centre of the bud stands slightly higher than the outside. Pinch off excess at base.

If you find this blend too soft to work with, leave out the transparent Fimo.

---

3 Pinch off four small pieces of thin Fimo and press round the bud as petals. Roll stem gently between your fingers to blend in and extend stem. Pinch off excess.
4 Carefully stick a length of florists' wire into the base – but don't squash the rose.
5 Stick wires into an old potato and harden roses in a cooling oven at 210°F (100°C) for 10 minutes. As the Fimo hardens it should contract to hold the wire. If a wire is still loose once hardened, apply a spot of glue to secure.
6 Trim stems to length and push carefully into mesh holes of canvas.
7 Use a pin to clear any paint-filled holes.

Silver Rose Bowl

A silver bowl filled with fresh roses looks good in any setting. Choose a large, low silver bead, sometimes called a rondel, for the bowl.

The Victorian rose was different from the hybrid tea we know today. It was smaller and less compact. It's easy to make a rose from Fimo, but an alternative is to use some dried Si roses which have been described by a supplier of miniature plants as the smallest variety available.

METHOD

1 To make bowl, trim a circle of embroidery canvas to fit over top of silver bead. Spray canvas silver. When dry glue in place.

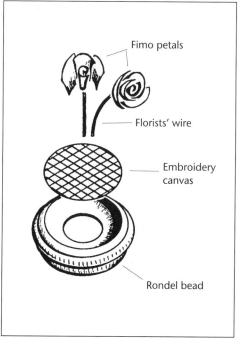

Fimo petals

Florists' wire

Embroidery canvas

Rondel bead

Materials

Large silver rondel bead

Embroidery canvas

Fimo: white, red, and transparent

Thin florists' wire

Paint: silver

Tacky glue

Regency Silver Tea Service

This set is based on a Regency design. It could also pass for Georgian because of the spout on the milk jug.

METHOD

TEAPOT

1 Glue washer to base of cushion bead. Glue bell cap on top of bead, over thread hole. Glue tiny bead on bell cap, to make lid handle.
2 Roll a small sausage in Milliput, slightly thicker at one end, for the spout. Poke a hole in the thinner end with a darning needle. Join the other end onto the pot, curving the spout.
3 Roll another sausage, slightly thicker at one end, for handle. Holding pot upside down, press thicker end of handle onto the pot opposite the spout. Turn the pot upright, allow the handle to fall into a curve and press base of handle to bottom of pot. Pinch off excess Milliput.

MILK JUG AND SUGAR BOWL

1 Fill in base of the ribbed beads with Milliput.
2 Make a small spout and handle for milk jug with Milliput, as for teapot.

3 Make two small handles for sugar bowl with Milliput.

FINISH

1 Paint all Milliput parts silver to blend with beads.
2 Mix salt with a little tacky glue, fill bowl and leave to dry.
3 Mix a drip of white acrylic paint with a little tacky glue, fill jug and leave to dry.
4 Remove excess fittings from brooch mount with pliers or snips.
5 Bend claws on pendant mounts to fit onto sides of tray. Glue in place with a tiny dot of superglue, followed by Araldite to secure firmly.

Materials

Large silver cushion bead

Silver ribbed ring beads x 2

Large silver washer or rivet x ½

Tiny plain bell cap

Tiny silver bead

Milliput

Paint: silver and white

Tacky glue

Table salt

Large brooch mount

Small pendant mount x 2

Superglue

Araldite

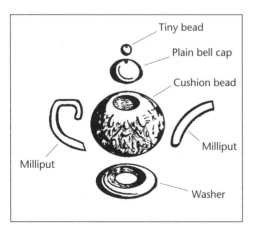

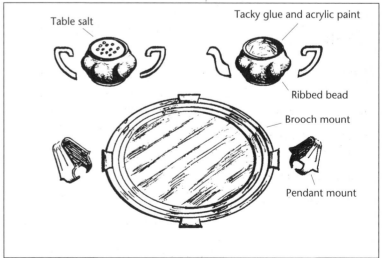

Porcelain Figurines

These figurines are made from white metal fairground figures, HO/OO scale, from a mail order supplier. There are also plastic railway models on the same scale. I find female figures are often more suitable for representing both sexes since they are smaller and more graceful.

METHOD

CUSTOMIZING FIGURES

1 Use a craft knife to pare down the figure if necessary. The lead alloy pares off very easily.

Stick the figure to a cotton reel, or similar, with Blu-Tack to make it easier to handle.

---

2 Press tiny pieces of Superfine Milliput to the figure to make a full skirt with a defined waist. Milliput can be textured with a pinpoint beforehand. Use the pinhead to blend the Milliput to the metal. Use the pinpoint to add folds to the skirt. Either press Milliput on in blobs or roll out very thin strips and drape around the figure. The latter is much easier to do with almost hardened Milliput. (To harden, place on the radiator for a few minutes.)

If the Milliput is reluctant to stick to the metal, a tiny dot of superglue will help.

---

3 Press the finished figurine onto a ball of Milliput to serve as a base. This can be pinched or textured to represent grass or rock.
4 Use a section of dried grape stem for a gnarled tree.
5 Use thin beading wire for swing ropes.

Here are some other ideas for modifying figures: stick a tiny piece of Milliput to the head for a bonnet or top hat; make a shepherd's crook from thick wire, bent to shape; flatten a piece of Milliput for a cape; give a gentleman a stick made from a cut down pin; disguise an out-of-period handbag with a muff.

PAINTING

1 Apply a coat of white acrylic or spray paint as a primer. Spray paint will retain more of the detail.
2 Leave the flesh parts white. Paint the clothes with acrylic paints. Study some examples of full-size painted ornaments, such as Meissen porcelain, for use of bright pastels like pink, yellow and orange.
3 Gild figures lightly with a fine gold marker pen. Leave to dry for 24 hours.
4 Coat figurines with clear nail varnish or polish, which blurs the paint to give an attractive porcelain finish – and don't forget to sign the base.

Materials

Packet of white metal figures, HO/OO scale

Superfine Milliput

Grape twig (not shown in illustration)

Thin wire

Spray primer: white

Acrylic paints

Fine marker pen: gold

Clear varnish

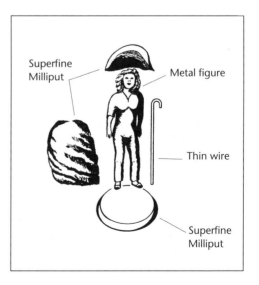

Superfine Milliput

Metal figure

Thin wire

Superfine Milliput

Materials

Small wooden building block

Thin picture frame moulding

Thin brass rod, ½in (1mm)

Medium brass rod, ³⁄₆₄in (1.2mm)

Belaying pin

Seed beads: gold and black

Thin aluminium or tin sheet

Small washer

Thin wood strip, ³⁄₁₆in (5mm)

Large brass cone (jewellery finding)

Half a brass rivet

Small brass washer

Small nickel washer

Snippet of brass tube, ³⁄₁₆in (5mm)

Tiny brass nail

Snippet of thin leather

Thin black plastic sheet, ½in (1mm)

Grip Wax

Tacky glue

Araldite

Superglue

Gramophone

The gramophone succeeded the phonograph at the turn of the century as a means of listening to recorded sound. The list of components for this project looks long, but they do go together in a straightforward way.

METHOD

BASE
1 Cut picture frame moulding to fit around base of block. Mitre edges. Glue frame to block.
2 Drill a ½in (1mm) hole in the centre of the block. Press in a snippet of medium brass rod.

HANDLE
1 Drill a ½in (1mm) hole in one side of the block near the top. Bend a length of thin brass rod as shown, right. Thread on gold seed bead and fix into the hole with Grip

Wax rather than glue. (This will allow the handle to turn.)
2 Snip the end off a belaying pin. Drill a tiny hole to fit rod in the centre of the belaying pin. Glue in place.

HORN
1 Glue half rivet to end of brass cone.
2 Bend a snippet of brass tube to a near right angle. Trim to about ⅜in (9.5mm) long and glue one end inside cone.
3 Glue a snippet of thin brass rod into the other end.
4 Glue the nickel washer, followed by the brass washer onto the thin rod.
5 Glue black seed bead to end of thin rod as a hand grip.

NEEDLE
1 Snip off and discard the top of the brass nail. Glue to nickel washer facing downwards.

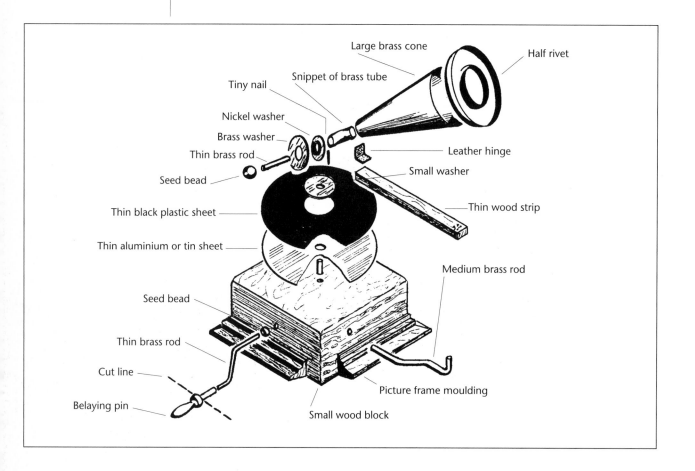

Large brass cone

Half rivet

Snippet of brass tube

Tiny nail

Nickel washer

Brass washer

Leather hinge

Thin brass rod

Small washer

Seed bead

Thin black plastic sheet

Thin wood strip

Thin aluminium or tin sheet

Medium brass rod

Seed bead

Thin brass rod

Cut line

Picture frame moulding

Belaying pin

Small wood block

ARM

1 Drill a ½in (1mm) hole in an adjacent side of the block. Bend a length of medium brass rod as shown, above. Fix into hole with Grip Wax to allow movement, as shown in illustration.
2 Cut a length of wood strip to join arm to horn. Drill a ½in (1mm) hole in one end and glue medium rod into hole.
3 Glue a snippet of leather to brass tube on horn and to other end of arm to act as a hinge. The needle can now be repositioned when desired.

TURNTABLE

1 Cut a circle in aluminium sheet a shade smaller than the base. Sand edge smooth.
2 Drill a central hole and glue turntable to base, over the medium rod.
3 Glue a small washer on top.

RECORDS

1 Cut circles of black acrylic sheet to the size of the base.
2 Grooves can be etched on with a sharp pin but there is an easier and more effective way using a mini drill and a sanding disc. Stick the record firmly onto the rubber backed sanding disc with a circle of double-sided tape. Press the rotating drill, and record, onto coarse sandpaper for a moment or two. Repeat for reverse.

Always be sure to wear both protective goggles and gloves when working with a mini drill.

---

3 Clamp the records together and fix into a vice. Drill a hole in the centre, the size of the central washer of the turntable.

CHAPTER ELEVEN

Oriental
Objets d'Art

2 Glue a thin black button to the base. Fill in thread holes of small domed button for lid. If it has no shank, add a plug of Milliput to underside so that it fits jar. Paint plug and thread holes black to match lid.

SCENTED JAR

1 Enlarge the pierced soapstone's thread hole using a round file or mini drill.
2 Glue brass washer to pierced bell cap to make a stand. Glue jar to stand.
3 Fill with tiny potpourri.

I used tiny fragments from the bottom of my dried flower box for the potpourri.

4 Use a shank button for the lid. Glue a tiny bead to the centre of the button for the handle.

SMALL JARS

1 Use the same method as for the scented jar, but with china beads. For lids use small plain bell caps with the thread hole filled with Milliput and painted to blend in. Make the bases from brass washers.

Oriental Jars

Attractive plastic, wood or soapstone beads make more realistic pots and vases if the thread hole is enlarged using a round file or mini drill. China beads will have to stay as they are. Scented jars were used to hold oils or flower petals.

METHOD

GINGER JAR

1 If the bead is plastic or wood (one of mine was described as cinnamon wood) clamp into a vice and drill out a larger hollow in the thread hole.

Materials

Oriental-style beads: plastic, wooden, china

Selection of bell caps

Selection of brass washers

Small domed black buttons

Small thin black buttons

Pierced soapstone bead

Milliput

Superglue

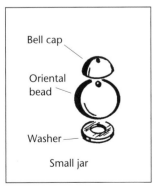

Bell cap

Oriental bead

Washer

Small jar

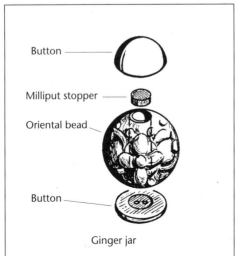

Button

Milliput stopper

Oriental bead

Button

Ginger jar

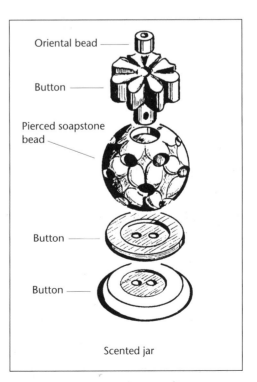

Oriental bead

Button

Pierced soapstone bead

Button

Button

Scented jar

Oriental Ornaments

Here is another example of appropriating components from other people's hobbies. War games suppliers stock a plethora of finely detailed cast metal alloy figures in varying scales. They are available by mail order and cost only a few pence each.

Here I turned an Indian elephant with a canopied seat (a howdah) and figures into an exotic planter by scraping the two passengers out of the howdah with a craft knife. Animal eyes set with tiny rhinestones look particularly effective. The two Samurai models shown in the photograph were sold under the description of 15mm models. They were decorated in a similar way to the elephant, and mounted on buttons.

METHOD

1 Adapt the model if necessary. Lead alloy is easily pared off with a craft knife. Spray

with a thin coat of primer.

***

The model will be far easier to handle if it is secured with Blu-Tack to a block of scrap wood or similar.

***

2 Use a fine, good quality brush for painting. Since the models are Eastern ornaments, indulge in rich and exotic colours rather than naturalistic ones.
3 Add a little gilding with gold marker pen.
4 Why not go mad and encrust the model with tiny rhinestones. Use the finest drill bit you have to make tiny dips to set stones in. Glue stones in with superglue.

***

To set a tiny rhinestone, chase it about till it lies face up. Moisten your finger tip and press it onto the stone. Apply a spot of Superglue into the setting using a pinhead then press the stone in, removing your finger as soon as it makes contact.

***

5 Allow paint to dry for 24 hours then spray finished model with clear lacquer.
6 Glue to button base.
7 Fill howdah with Blu-Tack, press on tea leaves for soil. Make a few holes with a needle and poke in the plant stems. I used dried asparagus fern sprayed green.

Materials

Suitable white metal alloy figure

Tiny rhinestones

Button, suitable for mount

Spray primer: white

Acrylic paints

Fine marker pen: gold or silver

Clear spray lacquer

Tea leaves

Blu-Tack

Dried fern

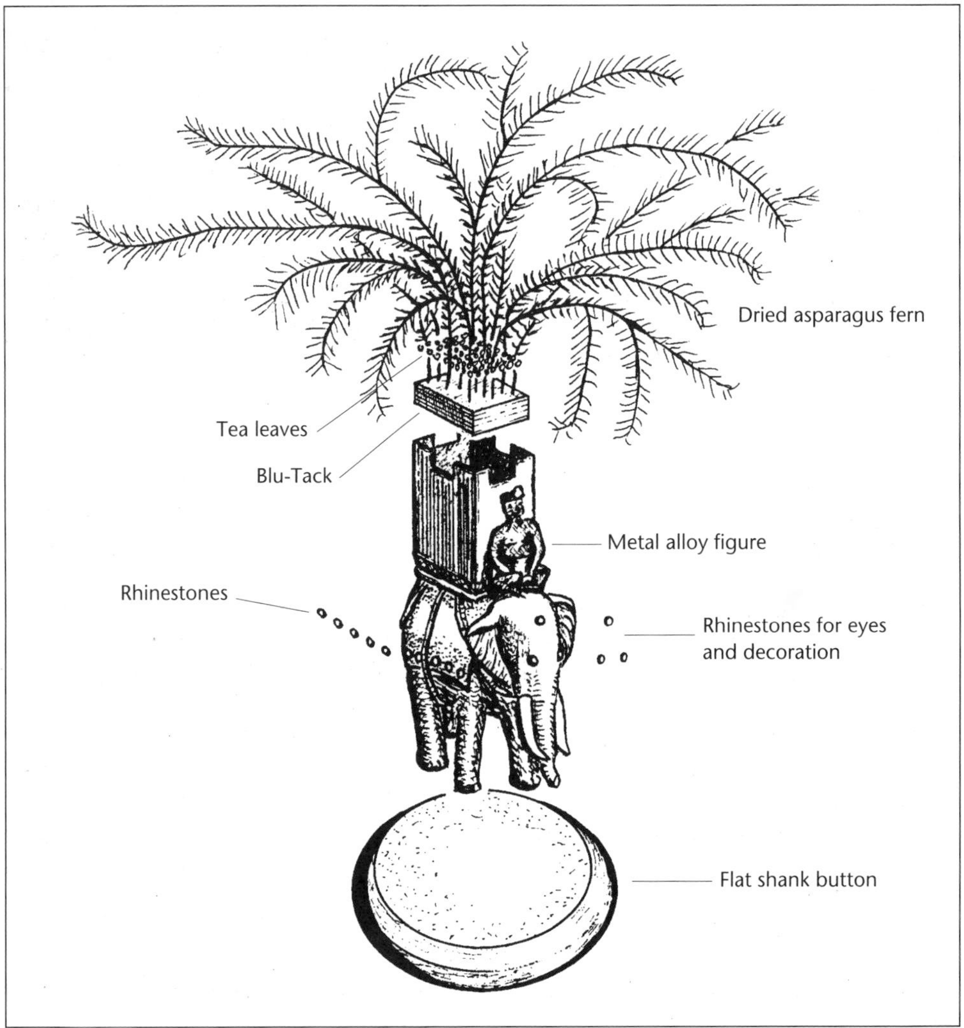

Dried asparagus fern

Tea leaves

Blu-Tack

Metal alloy figure

Rhinestones

Rhinestones for eyes and decoration

Flat shank button

Oriental Screen

I based this on a Victorian design which appeared in *Hampton and Sons Complete House Furnishings Catalogue* of 1894. It could equally well go into an Edwardian or Georgian setting. The original screen came hand painted, with cloth back and brocaded borders, measured 4ft 6in (137cm) and cost the princely sum of eight shillings and six pence, including carriage.

To make four panels you'll need a greetings card printed on front and back, or two cards of the same design. For backing I used thin wooden sheeting from a vegetable crate, about ⅛in (3mm) thick. Thick cardboard is an alternative but lacks the weight.

METHOD

PANELS

1 Divide the greetings cards into four equal panels.
2 Cut four matching panels from the wood sheet – I used power scissors. (The exact dimensions will depend on the size of the greetings card. For my screen, each panel measured 5½ x 1⅝in (140 x 41mm).)
3 Cut four pieces of fabric to fit over the panels with a ¾in (19mm) overlap.
4 Cover two panels with fabric, using spray mount. Press the overlaps neatly onto the other side, as flat as possible, so they won't show through the card front. These will be the end panels.
5 Do likewise with the remaining two panels, **but** leave one long side unstuck on each of these 'centre' panels.

HINGEING PANELS

1 Lay an end panel, covered side down, next to a partly covered centre panel with the open side facing away. Repeat with the two remaining panels.
2 Stick a thin strip of fabric over the join between one end panel and one centre panel. Turn the strip ends over to neaten – overlap will be visible at this stage. Repeat for second set.

3 Turn both sets of panels over so covered side shows. Place next to each other so that the two central panels expose inner wood.
4 Stick a thin fabric strip directly onto the wood. Tuck free ends of fabric from both central panels under, and glue over hinge strip to neaten.
5 Fold the screen in half at the central hinge and glue a thin fabric strip over the exposed wood on the opposite side.

As you work, ensure hinges give enough leeway for panels to fold up.

FACADE

1 Cut out the four panels from the greetings cards.

Materials

Thin wood sheet, about ⅛in (3mm)

Greetings cards, with Oriental-style design x 2

Plain cotton fabric

Thin embroidered braid

Tacky glue

Spray mount (optional)

A metal rule and craft knife will give a cleaner cut than scissors.

2 Apply glue or spray mount on the cards and press onto the screen panels in an appropriate order to make up a pattern.
3 Carefully, but quickly, paint a thin coat of French polish over the picture to give an antique appearance.

Don't do what I'm always tempted to do and give it two coats. If you put more than one coat of French polish on card the finish goes blobby.

4 Once dry, glue braid along top and bottom of screen. Tuck edges under card.

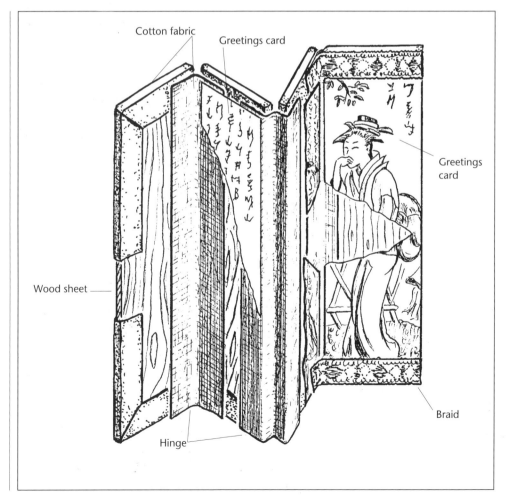

Gilt and Gemstone Bonsai

This ornament was inspired by the gemstone bonsai trees in the Thorne Rooms at the Chicago Art Institute, together with an eighteenth century Canton *famille rose* gilt and hardstone (gemstone) bonsai, seen in *Miller's Antique Price Guide*.

Save this project for a sunny day since glass glue dries instantly in strong sunlight. Bead and jewellery mail order suppliers stock tiny polished gemstones, as do many gift shops. Look out for tiny plastic domes labelled 'Little Gems'. The gilt pot is made from a cushion bead mounted on a jump ring and bell cap.

METHOD

FLOWERS

1 Cut a 6in (152mm) length of beading wire. Thread a yellow seed bead onto the middle of the wire and bend wire in half. Hold a quarter of the way down the wires and twist the bead about six times to secure it tightly. Repeat for four more stamens.

2 Pinch and twist all five wires together with thumb and forefinger just below twists. Collect half the wires together and twist loosely – this will be the stem.

3 Bend the other wire ends out to surround the seed bead stamens as supports for the petals.

4 Pierce a hole in a piece of scrap card. Thread the flower stem through the hole and secure with Blu-Tack to the back of the card. This makes the flower easier to handle.

5 Bend the five wire petal supports flat to the card. Away from sunlight, apply a dot of glass glue to each wire. Place a garnet stone onto each wire close to the central stamens. Lay in sunlight to harden, ensuring stones are positioned correctly.

6 Once dry, trim excess wires from petal ends. Make two or three further such flowers, following steps 1–5.

7 Glue single garnet stones to separate lengths of beading wire. These are buds – make three.

8 Glue single aventurine stones, for leaves, to separate lengths of beading wire in a similar manner. Make 12.

ASSEMBLY

1 Twist the stalk, bud and leaf wires firmly together to resemble a gnarled trunk. Trim off excess wires.

2 Fill pot with Milliput. Press trunk in and leave to harden.

3 Once secure, arrange stems of leaves, petals and buds to form an attractive shape.

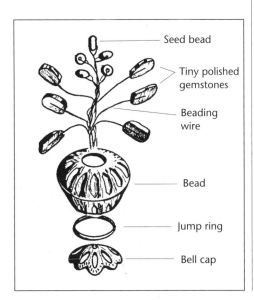

- Seed bead
- Tiny polished gemstones
- Beading wire
- Bead
- Jump ring
- Bell cap

Materials

Thin gilt beading wire

Packet of O size polished green gemstones, e.g. aventurine

Packet of O size polished red gemstones, e.g. garnet

Yellow seed beads

Suitably ornate gilt bead for pot, e.g. bead mounted on a bell cap

Glass glue

Milliput

Materials

Feathers x 7

Lid, for pot, or a cut
down wooden bead
(not shown in
illustration)

Tea leaves

Blu-Tack

Hair spray

Tacky glue

Acrylic paints: yellow
and brown

Thick marker pen:
green (ideally,
solvent-based)

Sago Palm

The sago palm is very slow growing, only putting out one new frond per year. I have made this one from feathers, which gives it a beautifully delicate appearance. Feathers which resemble fish bones work better than the fluffy sort.

I keep my feather collection in a large resealable transparent bag. I shake them about till I see the one I want, then fish it out. This stops them from floating away as I sort through them.

METHOD

1 Select six or seven untwisted feathers. (Colours needn't match.) Trim feathers evenly with manicure scissors to a graduated shape (*see* illustration).

**Fan feather out and cut from the tip
down to the quill.**

---

2 Give the frond a slight curve by gently running a scissor blade along the quill.
3 Lay on a piece of scrap paper and colour with a thick green marker pen on both sides. (Don't worry if it all sticks together.)
4 Once dry, smooth the feather out and spray with hair spray. Separate the spines evenly with a dressmakers' pin.
5 Paint a thin yellow line down the centre of each frond using a fine paintbrush and acrylic paint. If you make a mistake, dab the colour off immediately with a damp cotton wool bud.
6 Collect fronds into a bunch. Apply a little glue at the base of the stems. Roll between your thumb and forefinger until they stick together to form one stem.
7 Shape an oval ball of Milliput for nut base. Press stem into the centre and arrange fronds.
8 Push base into Blu-Tack, push into pot.
9 Make small angled cuts with a craft knife all the way around nut. Make opposite angle cuts over these to produce a rough texture. When hardened, paint brown.
10 Press tea leaves onto Blu-Tack for soil.

Trimmed feather fronds

Yellow spine

Milliput

CHAPTER TWELVE

Soft Furnishings

Towel

I made this towel from a snippet of old towelling headband.

METHOD

1 Turn two opposite edges of towelling under about ⅟₁₆in (1.5mm) and loosely hem.
2 Thread ribbon evenly through holes in lace. Sew lace to two remaining edges of towel to conceal cut end.
3 Fold hemmed edges to meet in centre of towel and drape over rail.

Materials

Fine towelling or similar, about 3 x 3in (76 x 76mm)

Lace trimming with holes

Thin ribbon

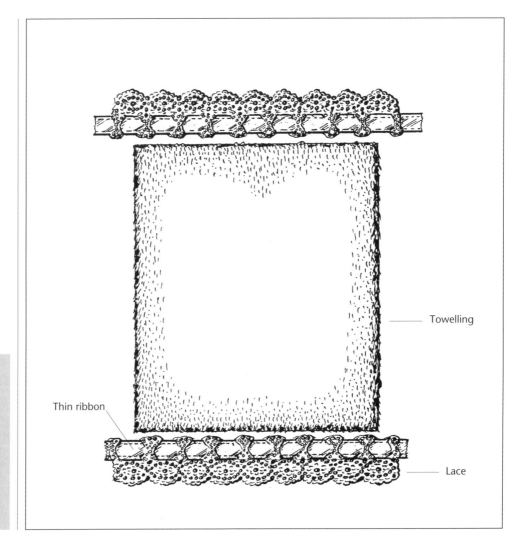

Towelling

Thin ribbon

Lace

Draped Table

The Tudors draped their most precious carpets over tables, to keep them off the floor. The carpet in turn was protected by a linen 'toilette' (a trimmed cloth). These table-carpets often matched the bed curtains. The Georgians also used fine carpet as table covering. If a table could be draped, the Victorians draped it, usually with several layers. Victorian prudery developed to a point where legs of any description were thought best skirted.

A collection of household lids and tops are under some of my draped tables. I can't always bring myself to obscure lovingly polished and marbled tables. The choice of lid will depend on the size of the table required. I chose mine to fit the lace doily.

METHOD

1 Wrap a strip of paper around the side of the lid and tape in place temporarily.
2 Measure from the centre of the lid to the base. (There is a tiny bump in the centre of most aerosol lids which is the mid-point.)
3 Lay the silk flat and draw a light pencil circle on it using the above measurement as the radius.

Rather than use a compass, try to find a suitably sized round object to use as a template, e.g. a saucer.

---

4 Cut out and apply a tiny line of tacky glue (or fray check if you have some) to the edge of the silk to prevent fraying.

Be sure to use sharp scissors to make a clean cut in silk.

---

5 Sew lace trimming to edge, or use spray mount.
6 Drape silk cloth over lid. Pin down at four diametrically opposed points, through trimming, into paper, then pin down the spaces in-between.
7 Once draping is arranged, pin doily in place over the top. Spray both liberally with starch and leave to dry.
8 Once dry, remove pins and pull out paper from underneath drape.

If the table is to hold a lamp or candle, thread the bulb wires through a hole in the doily or weave of the fabric (no need to cut) and run the wires down the side of the lid and through the floor.

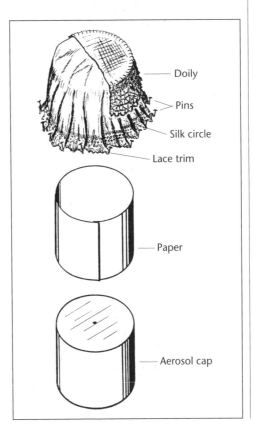

- Doily
- Pins
- Silk circle
- Lace trim
- Paper
- Aerosol cap

Materials

Large cap or lid, e.g. aerosol cap

Silk or tapestry fabric

Lace trim (Victorian setting only)

Small doily, linen or lace

Scrap paper

Tacky glue

Spray starch

Materials

Thin red crushed velvet

Cotton guipure edging, 1yd (91cm)

Red tasselled cord, e.g. tassel from greetings card

Brass tubing, ⅟₁₆in (1.5mm)

Gilt jump rings, ⁹⁄₃₂in (7mm) x 10

Screw-eyes x 2

Brass pins x 2

Permanent solvent-based marker pen: red

Tacky glue

Chenille Cloths and Portière

Chenille was a type of crushed velvet popular in the nineteenth century for making the red plush tablecloths that were draped over the parlour table. The matching portière curtain was to keep out draughts. In working class houses there was sometimes no door, just a curtain. Cotton guipure lace edging resembles Victorian bobble edging. It's generally white so use a solvent-based marker pen to colour it.

As for the tie-back, I made good use of the fancy tassels sometimes found on greetings cards.

METHOD

TABLECLOTH

1 Choose a table for the cloth to cover. Find a plate or bowl of a suitable size for table.

Draw around the shape carefully and cut from velvet.

2 Edge with guipure trimming.

MANTEL CLOTH

1 Cut a length of fabric 2in (51mm) longer than the mantel shelf.

2 Drape the fabric over the mantelpiece and cut to length allowing the cloth to drape over about 1in (25.5mm).

3 Pin the wrong side of the triangular overlap and sew up underneath so the cloth fits the mantel shelf.

4 Sew guipure trim around draped edge.

PORTIÈRE CURTAIN

1 Cut a length of ⅟₁₆in (1.5mm) brass tubing, 1in (25.5mm) longer than the width of the door.

2 Cut a piece of fabric 1in (25.5mm) longer and 2in (51mm) wider than the door.

3 Stitch guipure edging along one long side.

4 Neatly hem the top and bottom and remaining side.

5 Stitch the 10 jump rings to the top hem, spacing them evenly.

6 Thread the jump rings onto the brass tube.

7 Screw the two screw-eyes into the door lintel (surround above door) if door opens inwards, or into the door itself if door opens outwards. Ensure they are level.

8 Thread the ends of the brass tube into the screw-eyes. Glue a brass pin into each end to secure in place. (If you prefer, use Grip Wax for a temporary join.)

9 Gather the curtain back to the hinge side of the door (with running stitch) and tie with the tasselled cord.

SHAPING

1 Spray all three items liberally with starch. Shape the cloths on the table and mantel shelf, arrange the curtain in folds and leave to dry.

Cushions

Upholstered furniture and cushions were by no means common until the eighteenth century and then only in wealthy households. Tudor cushions were adorned with fat tassels.

Wide, embroidered haberdashery braid makes excellent cushions in no time. As an alternative, use transfer emulsion to transfer pictures of embroidery to linen (*see* page 7).

METHOD

1 Choose a section of braid with a suitable central pattern and cut two squares. Sew up three edges, right sides together.
2 Turn out, stuff lightly with wadding and sew up fourth side.
3 To make cording, twist a length of embroidery silk until it coils. Press one end of cording inside cushion and, using a strand of matching thread, stitch cording around cushion edges. Finish corners in a tassel or a twist.

Materials

Fabric

Embroidery silks

Lace trim

Wadding

Georgian Festoon Blinds

Georgian windows were high and narrow. Simple fine gauze hangings were often the only curtains. After the 1720s, festoon curtains were fashionable in important rooms but the ruching was never very regular. The workings were hidden behind a decorative carved and gilded cornice. Each window would have had its own festoon, adjusted by long cords.

Materials

Large wood or plastic moulding (Queen Anne leaf from a hardware shop)

Silk or similar fabric

Cord

Fringe trim

Screw-eyes x 3

Jump rings x 30

Thin silk ribbon

Spray paint: off-white

Thin marker pen: gold

METHOD

CORNICE

1 Check moulding fits window. Prime moulding and paint off-white. Volkswagen pastel white spray paint is a suitable shade.

2 Gild lightly with a thin gold marker pen. Set aside to dry.

FESTOON BLIND

1 Cut fabric to the length of the window and the width of the cornice. Turn long edges under and hem lightly.

2 Sew silk ribbon down both long sides and down centre.

3 Sew about 10 jump rings evenly spaced to each ribbon.

4 Tie a knot in a length of cord (about twice length of window), fray one end into a tassel and sew knot to base of blind. Thread cord through jump rings. Repeat for two remaining pulls.

5 Edge base with fringe trim. I used cut down lampshade trim.

6 Fix two screw-eyes to base of cornice at either edge and the third screw-eye to the centre.

7 Thread one cord through first screw-eye, thread that plus central cord through central eye and all three cords through end eye. Tie cords together and trim to equal lengths. Fray and trim end into a tassel.

8 Glue top of blind to back of cornice, below screw-eyes.

9 Spray blind with starch, draw up, arrange folds and leave to dry.

10 Fix cornice to top of window with Sticky Fixers (or use Blu-Tack for a temporary joint).

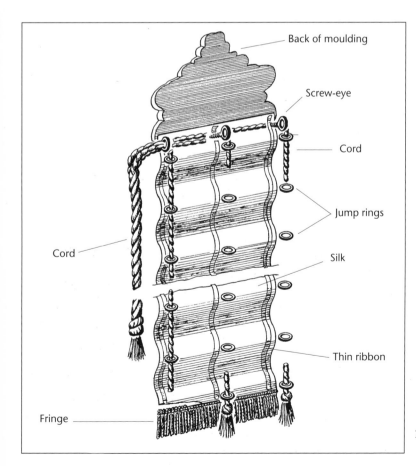

Back of moulding

Screw-eye

Cord

Jump rings

Silk

Thin ribbon

Cord

Cord

Fringe

Tudor Bed Hangings

I was inspired to make the Tudor bed in Bedroom Accessories (*see* page 63), by this rich gold cotton fabric. It was a little too bright to resemble natural dyes but this was soon remedied by a soaking in strong black coffee.

Since the Tudor house was not separated into rooms as such and indoor heating was practically non-existent, the drapes performed the dual purpose of providing privacy and keeping out draughts. Suitable colours for the drapes include dark red, dark green or gold.

METHOD

CURTAINS

1 Measure top of canopy to floor. Cut fabric adding 1in (25.5mm) for seam allowance. Turn over and hem top to accommodate twine for gathering.
2 Stitch trimming to bottom edge. Make four hangings.
3 Fix screw-eyes into corners of canopy. (The eyes in the front posts help to secure the skewers in place.) Thread twine onto darning needle and then thread through back left screw-eye, first curtain, half of second curtain, front left screw-eye, rest of second curtain, half of third curtain, front right screw-eye, rest of third curtain, fourth curtain and back right screw-eye. Secure both ends of the twine tautly. Tie hangings back neatly with thick cord.
4 Stick trimming inside canopy with double-sided tape.

COUNTERPANE

1 Cut fabric big enough to drape bed with mattress already fitted. (A piece of thick packing foam cut to size will serve as a mattress.)
2 Pin thin wadding to inside of counterpane, where top of mattress will be. Back the counterpane with thin cotton and pin in place.

Placing the wadding in the centre helps the counterpane drape more realistically.

3 To quilt counterpane, I used gold thread and chain stitch and followed pattern on fabric. I found it easier to do this by hand but you could use a sewing machine if you prefer.
4 Hem top edge back. Sew trimming to other three edges.

BOLSTER

1 Sew a tube of fabric, wrong side out. Cut two 1in (25.5mm) circles (draw around a coin or bottle cap). Sew one circle to one end and turn right side out. Stuff firmly with cotton wool.
2 Tuck in other end and sew in other circle, hiding the stitches. Sew a tassel to either end. Double a length of embroidery silk or gold thread. Use this thread to sew to bolster end. Tie a binding knot around both ends, pull to secure and trim tassel to size.

DRAPING

1 Arrange curtains, pin in place and spray with starch. Remove pins when dry.

'Ostrich plumes' (use gosling feathers or similar curled on a scissor blade) can be fixed into the finials as a finishing touch.

Materials

Lightweight cotton fabric

Trimming

Thin twine

Screw-eyes x 4

Wadding

Cotton wool

CHAPTER THIRTEEN

Fireplace Accessories

Hedgehog

I once overheard a customer in a dolls' house shop ask urgently, 'Where can I get a hedgehog?' Apparently, the essential fireside accessory for the fashionable country folk of the 1600s was a hedgehog. They ate more creepy crawlies than they brought with them as well as any scraps from the table: a kind of living Hoover.

You won't find a casuarina cone lying about unless you live in Australia or Asia, but you can find them at craft or florist suppliers.

METHOD

1 Sand off just under half the cone, lengthways.
2 Paint prickles a mixture of browns and black. Add a few highlights in white to tips of prickles.
3 Paint snout and underside dark brown.
4 Paint eyes and tip of snout black, and then varnish to appear moist.

Materials

Casuarina cone (craft or florist supplier)

Acrylic paint: browns, black and white

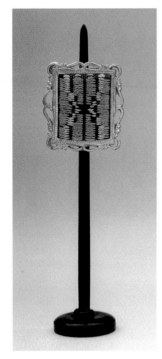

Georgian Fire Screen

A piece of tapestry or embroidery was often used to decorate a fire screen. You might like to embroider over a small cotton print. To represent Berlin work (a type of large embroidery with a coarser yarn), cut a suitable section from tapestry fabric or braid.

The original fire screen was positioned high up on a stand, its main function being to protect the Georgian lady's complexion from the fierce heat of the fire.

METHOD

1 Snip the crossbar out of the buckle with power scissors and file down rough edges.
2 Trim cardboard to fit into the centre of the buckle, but don't fit in yet.
3 Fix embroidered fabric to the cardboard using spray mount. Trim to size and fold over edges to neaten.
4 Back with a snippet of linen and fit into buckle.

Don't glue embroidery in if you want the option of changing the design at a later date.

---

5 Trim paintbrush handle to about 4¾in (108mm).
6 Blank out any lettering on the brush with matching paint.
7 Glue the thicker end of the paintbrush handle into the large button base with Araldite. Secure with a thin sausage of Milliput. When dry paint and varnish Milliput to match pole.
8 Bend two strips of thin brass onto back of screen to fit snugly over pole. Glue ends to frame. Ideally the strips should allow for some adjustment up and down.

Materials

Thin paintbrush handle

Large button

Medium belt buckle, square or round

Piece of embroidered fabric

Cardboard

Thin linen

Thin brass strip

Milliput

Spray mount

Araldite

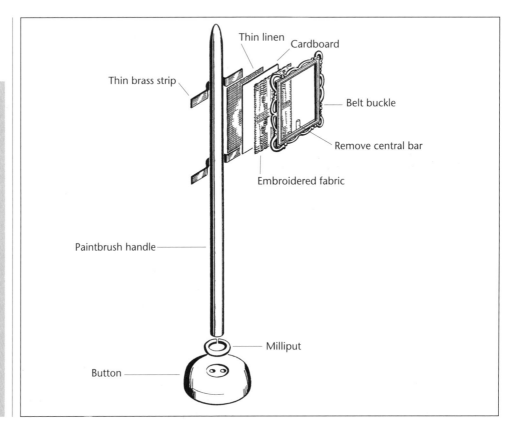

Brass Fire Guard

Years ago I read in a dolls' house book that small metal mesh purses, which were fashionable in the 1970s, made excellent ready-made fire guards. I finally came across one which I'd have paid anything for at a car boot sale. Excitedly, I got it home, made the slight modifications, set it in front of my nursery fireplace and . . . was rather disappointed. Each to their own.

Here is my suggestion for making a fire guard, based on a late Victorian design. It is simply a case of making the appropriate bends in the right places along the brass rod. Try practising the bends first on a 12in (30.5cm) length of garden wire.

METHOD

FRAME

1 The frame is made up of a brass rod, 12in (30.5cm), bent into shape. There are 10 bends plus one joint (*see* view, over page111). Begin at the shorter joint as marked on view and twist a right angle.

2 Twist two matching acute (shallow) angles for the foot. Twist an obtuse (wide) angle to clip around the first right-angled bend.

3 Bend two matching right angles for top two corners of the guard.

4 Make four bends for a second foot to match first foot, finishing with a right angle.

5 Bend the ends to meet each other. Snip off any excess rod.

Materials

Thin brass rod, ³⁄₆₄in (1.2mm)

Square of net or tulle, preferably cotton

Two decorative scrolls (or large eye from hook and eye fastener)

Thin brass rod, pliable

Pierced bell caps, small and medium

Gilt leaves x 2

Tacky glue

Araldite

Spray paint: gold

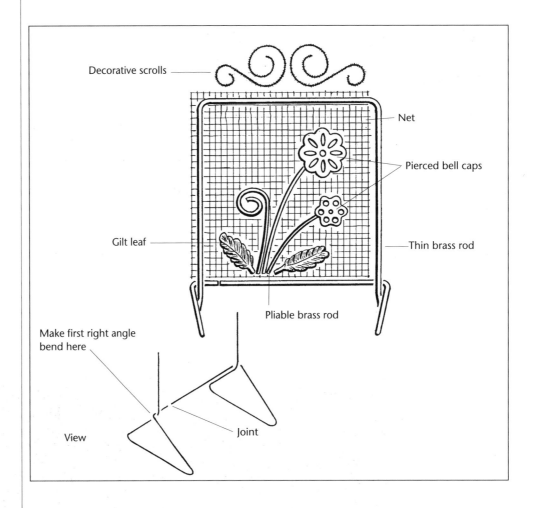

Make the screen as symmetrical as possible. Use your eye as a judge; it's difficult to measure curves.

---

6 File rod ends flat and apply Araldite to joint. Tie the guard's legs together with thread while the glue dries (elastic bands distort the joint). Once completely dry, snip thread off.

MESH

1 Spray net (cut to slightly larger than frame) with several coats of gold spray paint, on both sides. (I used a piece of old net curtain.) Once dry, paint will stiffen net.
2 Cut one straight side. Spread tacky glue over frame, line net up with base of frame and press onto glue. Stretch net tautly over frame before it dries.
3 Once dry, cut excess net away from three remaining sides, close to frame, with manicure scissors.

DECORATION

1 Any thin gilt findings can be used. I flattened the bell caps and stuck them onto the net with tacky glue. I then added some flat gilt leaves and joined these with bent thin brass rod, glued in place.
2 Add the scrolled stem by bending a short section of brass rod into a flat coil.
3 Glue two scrolls on top of the frame using Araldite. As an alternative, use eye of a large hook and eye fastener, opened up a little – this looks just as effective.

Art Nouveau Fireplace

Not content with the materials generally available to the enthusiastic miniaturist, where possible I like to appropriate components from other hobbies.

I spotted the Art Nouveau-style finding which inspired this project in a catalogue stocking filigrees for Egg Decorators. The grate is brass gallery trim, intended for model shipbuilding. The tile pictures were cut from a sumptuous mail order tile catalogue.

METHOD

SURROUND

1 Cut a section of brass sheet 3½ x 2½in (89 x 63.5mm). Adjust measurements to fit your surround. Fasten filigree temporarily with Blu-Tack (I trimmed mine down slightly) to centre top of sheet. Mark out a central panel leaving two sides of equal width. Score lightly down both lines with a craft knife. Bend to shape to fit surround.

2 Use a felt-tip pen to mark intended position of decorative filigree and two thin brass strips either side of central panel.

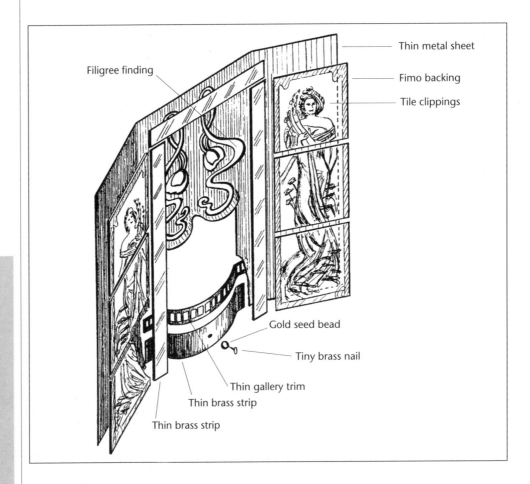

Filigree finding

Thin metal sheet

Fimo backing

Tile clippings

Gold seed bead

Tiny brass nail

Thin gallery trim

Thin brass strip

Thin brass strip

Materials

Wood fireplace surround, available from specialist dolls' house suppliers (not shown in illustration)

Thin metal sheet, 0.008in

Art Nouveau-style filigree finding

Thin metal gallery trim

Thin brass strip

Gold seed bead

Tiny brass nail

Catalogue clippings of tiles

Fimo: transparent

Araldite

Spray mount (or tacky glue)

Spray paint: matt black

Clear water-based varnish, e.g. Decal-it

Cut carefully round shape with power scissors and discard central section.

If you have any old manicure scissors use these to cut brass sheet. They are less cumbersome than power scissors.

3 Gently bend the flue section up and out slightly with pliers. Glue the thin brass strips to both sides of opening then glue on the filigree, bending to match the flue. Glue another piece of thin brass strip across top, over filigree.

4 Bend another section of thin brass strip to fit base of opening, glue in place. Drill a tiny ½in (1mm) hole in the centre. Glue in place. Bend and glue a section of gallery trim on top of brass strip.

5 Spray assembly with primer, followed by several thin coats of matt black.

6 Once dry, glue a gold seed bead onto tiny brass nail, press nail into hole in brass strip for grate knob.

TILES

1 Cut out strips of tile clippings using a craft knife and steel rule. Roll out a thin layer of transparent Fimo, lay tile strips on top and score round with craft knife. Remove tile strips, harden Fimo in a cooling oven.

2 Fix tile strips to Fimo strips with spray mount, apply a coat of clear water-based varnish and cut into separate tiles with a craft knife.

3 Glue in place on surround. (I mixed up the two central tiles with the result that the figures in my tiles now appear to have three arms each!)

4 Fix whole assembly to back of wood surround with Blu-Tack.

Lantern Clock

Lantern clocks changed very little from the seventeenth to the nineteenth century. All components for the miniature should be brass (or gilt). Originally, these clocks were wall mounted, but if the clock is to stand on a shelf or on furniture, the weights can be left off.

METHOD

1 Cut a strip of brass ½in (12.5mm) deep using power scissors. Mark four ⁵⁄₁₆in (8mm) lines along top and bottom. Gently score along these lines with a craft knife.

2 Fold the brass strip, score lines on the outside, to make a box. Trim off excess brass and stick overlap inside with Araldite.

3 Cut a ¹⁄₁₆in (1.5mm) strip of brass. Cut strip in two and drill a tiny hole, ¹⁄₃₂in (1mm), through both centres. Press a gold seed bead followed by a gold ball onto the dressmakers' pin, then press pin through two holes in strips. Press the large bell cap onto pin last, underneath brass strips. Apply glue inside bell cap to secure pin.

4 Cut four pieces of square wood strip to fit each corner of brass box. Drill a tiny ¹⁄₃₂in (1mm) hole in all four ends (use a vice to do this). Trim and glue the four ends of the two brass strips into box corners, then glue four wood strips into each corner (drill-hole at base).

5 Press a tiny brass nail into the top of each brass and wood corner. (Leave nail a little raised.)

6 Press four gold balls onto four tiny nails. Press one into each of the four holes in wood strips inside the body.

7 Glue filigree scrolls to back and front of clock body top.

8 Glue decorative washer to front of clock body. Glue a seed bead in centre of washer.

9 Cut a section of filigree from a suitable finding to make an hour hand (or use a

decorative wristwatch hour hand). Press tiny brass nail through end of filigree. Press into central seed bead.

Add a minute hand for eighteenth and nineteenth century lantern clocks.

---

10 Fill cord end caps with Milliput. Once

dry, paint ends gold. Fix to a length of chain about 4in (102mm) long, with a large link.

11 Glue the two tiny washers onto each end of a second length of chain about 2½in (64mm) long.

12 Glue chain centres asymmetrically (unevenly) to inside back of clock.

Materials

Brass sheet, 0.005in

Wood strip, ⅛in (3mm) square

Tiny gold balls x 5

Tiny gold seed beads x 4

Dressmakers' pin

Tiny brass nails x 8

Small decorative filigrees x 2

Large plain bell cap

Decorative washer

Snippet of filigree

Gilt trace chain

Cord end caps x 2

Tiny washers x 2

Large jump rings x 2

Araldite

Paint: gold

Milliput

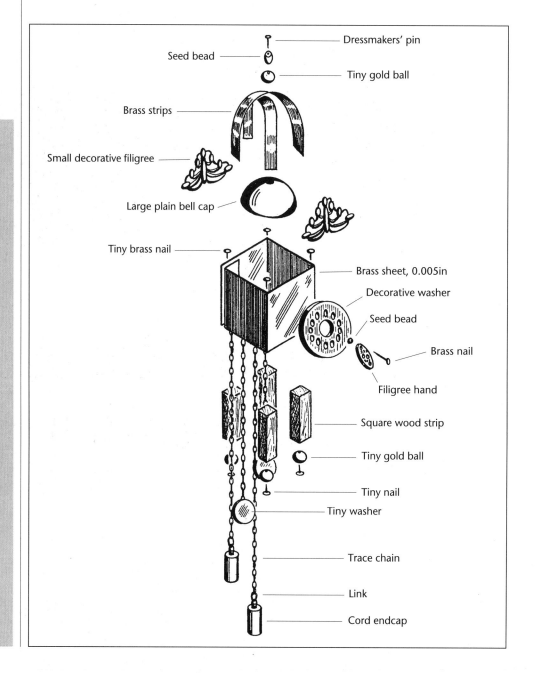

CHAPTER FOURTEEN

Dining Room Accessories

Materials

Brass rod, ⅟₁₆in
(1.5mm)

Brass beads x 2

Large links, 'S'
shaped x 2

Hollow brass shank
button

Skewer

Small wooden bead

Milliput

Superglue

Table Gong

I generally favour small models so that I can
squeeze more into my room settings. You
might like to make a larger version of this
gong if you have a grander hall.

Try to find an old brass shank button that is
old and worn; otherwise the gong will appear
never to have been banged.

METHOD

GONG

1 Snip the shank off the button with power
scissors. Carefully prise off the metal
backing and discard.

**To remove back, get a grip on the
opening where the shank was fixed
with thin-nosed pliers. Twist and pull
firmly – the back should come away
cleanly.**

---

2 Straighten the edge of the remaining part
slightly, all the way around.
3 Bend a length of ⅟₁₆in (1.5mm) brass rod to
fit round gong using tube benders if you
have some.
4 Stick the two links onto back of gong with
Milliput.

**I used 'S' shaped links. If using oval
links you may prefer to drill two tiny
holes in the gong.**

---

5 Once the Milliput is hardened, thread
links onto the rod. Trim ends of the rods
to size and mount on brass beads with
Milliput.
6 Cut a length of rod to fit between legs,
above brass beads. Glue in place using
Araldite.

HAMMER

1 Push the point of the skewer into thread
hole of wooden bead. Snip off protruding tip
and file smooth.
2 Snip skewer to size and sand down end.

**Use a couple of pieces of Grip Wax on
the feet to stand the gong up.**

Large links ———— S S   Wooden bead

Shank button

Brass rods

Brass bead

Skewer

Biscuit Tin and Barrel

Tinned biscuits became available during the 1870s. A picture often decorated the lid. A good place to find such a picture clipping is a greetings card catalogue. At the start of the twentieth century tins began to bear a maker's name, such as Huntley and Palmer.

METHOD

TIN

1 Trace the two patterns, (*see* over), onto paper.
2 Lightly glue lid pattern onto a corner of tin sheet. Cut out with power scissors.

3 Score firmly along fold lines with a metal rule and craft knife.
4 Damp down the paper pattern, peel off and discard.
5 Clip into the solid line of each corner-square (*see* illustration, over page).
6 Fold back each corner-square and fold down each side with small pliers.

If you only have serrated pliers, bind jaws with sticking plaster to prevent marking the tin.

---

7 Form into a box shape, tucking corner-squares inside. Carefully trim any uneven overlaps.
8 Repeat steps 1–7 for base of tin.
9 Trim and glue picture to lid.

10 Line tin with greaseproof paper.

BARREL

1 Drill out central thread hole of wooden bead.

2 Sand disc bead to fit over or inside barrel for a lid.

3 Glue tiny wooden bead or belaying pin to lid for a handle.

4 Stain and coat with French polish.

BISCUITS

1 Mix a variety of colours to look like biscuit doughs from mixtures of white, yellow and brown Fimo. Use brown and white for a standard biscuit colour and just brown for a chocolate colour. Add yellow for a paler biscuit.

2 Roll out dough and cut out square and rectangular biscuits with a craft knife. Prick centres with a pin to look like fork pricks.

3 Use thick brass tubing, ⅚in (8mm), to cut out circular biscuits.

A tiny flower cutter, sold by cake decorating suppliers, is useful as a fancy biscuit cutter.

---

4 Decorate biscuits with a string of brown Fimo as piping. Stick some together with a contrasting colour filling.

5 Harden in a cooling oven for 10 minutes at 270°F (130°C).

6 Coat some biscuits with clear varnish and sprinkle with salt to give a sugared effect.

7 Macaroons can have sesame seeds added to look like almonds.

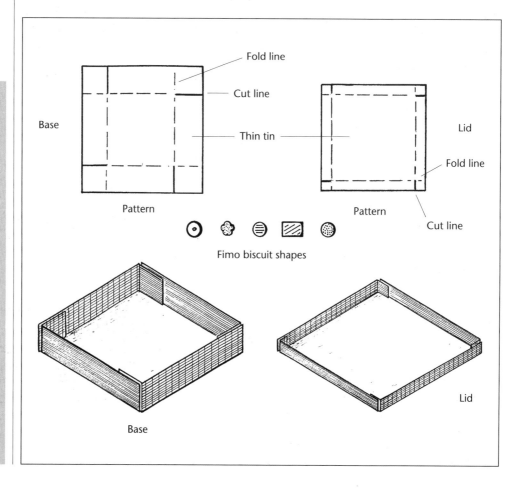

Fimo biscuit shapes

Silver Bonbon Dishes with Bonbons and Creams

You can make any sweetmeat in keeping with the period to go into these nineteenth century bonbon dishes. I chose lemon bonbons and peppermint creams.

METHOD

DISHES

1 Snip off (or fill in) thread holes from scallop shells.

2 Snip off foot shape from earring fastener just below loop. (Save screw findings for making oil lamps: *see* page 146.) Bend the foot into a right angle at the 'ankle', using pliers.

Components can be silver-plated before assembly if required.

---

3 Roll six tiny balls of Milliput. Press three onto the back of each scallop, evenly spaced. Press leg of a foot into each ball. Carefully stand dish on its feet on a flat surface and check it is straight before leaving Milliput to harden.

4 Once hardened, paint Milliput silver to

resemble solder.

5 Spray dishes with clear lacquer to prevent tarnishing.

LEMON BONBONS

1 Mix a speck of yellow with a small amount of transparent Fimo. Roll into a thin length.

2 Chop into small segments and roll each segment into a ball the size of a seed bead.

3 Harden in a cooling oven for 10 minutes.

4 Once hardened, liberally dust with talc. Place in dish with a little more talc.

PEPPERMINT CREAMS

1 Mix a speck of green Fimo with transparent to make very pale green.

2 Roll two thin lengths of pale green and transparent Fimo. Slice into thin rounds.

3 Harden in a cooling oven for 10 minutes.

Materials

Scallop shell findings (metal, plastic or shell) x 2

Screw-back earring fasteners x 6

Fimo: transparent, yellow and green

Talcum powder

Silver paint

Clear spray lacquer

Milliput

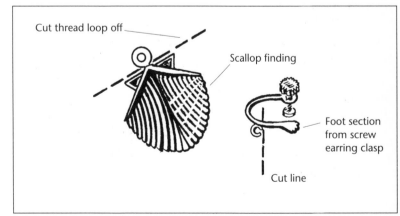

Cut thread loop off

Scallop finding

Foot section from screw earring clasp

Cut line

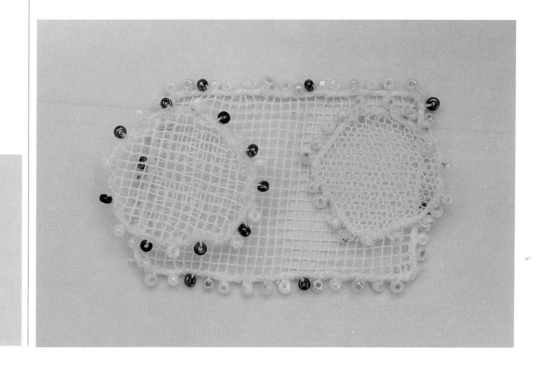

Materials

Soft netting

Selection of seed beads

Cotton thread

Crochet thread

Spray starch

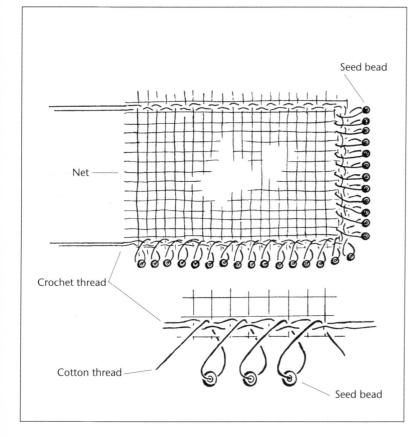

Seed bead

Net

Crochet thread

Cotton thread

Seed bead

Beaded Covers

Decorative beaded covers used to keep flies away from pots, jugs and trays of food. Choose fine cotton or soft nylon net in preference to stiff tulle. Old doilies and net curtains are a good source of cotton netting. Assorted balls of old crochet thread for edging are often available in charity shops.

METHOD

1 For a round cover, draw around a small coin and cut out a circle in net.

2 Stitch a border of crochet thread around the outside using a simple overstitch. Try to catch the snipped net threads in with the stitching to prevent fraying.

3 Stitch around a second time, this time threading on seed beads (*see* illustration). Tidy any loose threads by catching them under the stitches.

4 For tray cover, cut a rectangle from net to fit your tray, then repeat steps 1–3.

5 Spray covers with starch, drape over tray or bowl and leave to dry.

Pepper Mills

Pepper mills were introduced at the end of the nineteenth century. These pepper mills work only in that their handles turn. Use nickel or silver-plated findings to make the cut glass and silver mill, and wooden beads to make the other.

Glass and Silver Mill

METHOD

1 Glue crystal bead onto bell finding (I cut down top of bell finding a little.) Glue thick washer onto crystal bead. Set aside to dry.

Level the thread holes up with a lightly greased pin.

---

2 Thread a pin through tiny ball bead, spacer bar and thin washer. Set aside.
3 Thread a pin smeared with glue through the second tiny bead and into the other end of the spacer bar. Set aside to dry.

Place a piece of non-stick paper onto a pincushion and press pins into pincushion till dry. I use the paper that backs sticky labels.

---

4 Once dry, snip pin to size with power

Materials

Glass and Silver Mill

Bell-shaped finding

Medium crystal bead

Small thick washer

Small thin washer

Tiny ball bead

Small spacer bar

Dressmakers' pins x 2

Tiny wooden bead

Araldite

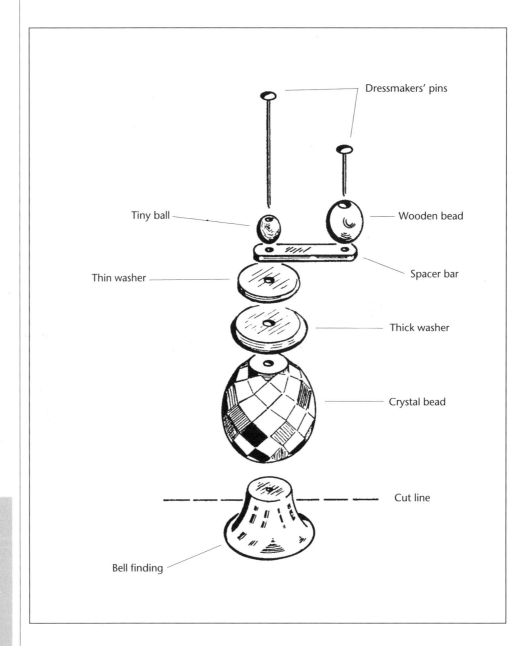

Dressmakers' pins

Tiny ball

Wooden bead

Spacer bar

Thin washer

Thick washer

Crystal bead

Cut line

Bell finding

Materials

Wooden Mill

Wooden lice bead

Small disc bead

Tiny eye from hook and eye fastener

Tiny eyelet

Tiny wooden beads x 2

Dressmakers' pin

Medium ribbed wooden bead

Tiny brass nail

scissors. Fit into mill body. Mill should rotate on mill body when turned by handle.

Wooden Mill

METHOD

1 Sand down wooden lice bead to fit onto small disc. Drill a tiny hole in the side of the wooden lice.

2 Snip down the tiny eye from hook and eye fastener. Glue into hole in lice. Push tiny eyelet into eye hole. Glue tiny wooden bead onto eyelet and press a cut-down brass nail into thread hole of bead. Set aside to dry.

3 Thread remaining tiny wooden bead, mill assembly and ribbed wooden bead, for base, onto a dressmakers' pin and snip off excess.

Clarice Cliff Tea Set

Clarice Cliff ceramics first appeared in the 1920s. She is best known for her later work using the bold, geometric Art Deco designs characteristic of the 1930s. This design is an interpretation of her hand painted 'Tennis' pattern. The full-size originals are collectors' pieces. Make four or six place settings depending on how many buttons you find. Buy up plenty of thin metal buttons when you come across them, as they usually don't cost much.

METHOD

CUPS

1 Using power scissors, cut a strip of aluminium slightly smaller than the height of the bell finding, for the handles. Snip several tiny triangles from this strip, and select the best six.

If the triangles curl up, flatten them with pliers.

---

2 Glue a triangular handle to each bell finding using tweezers. (Cup handles should not have hole.)

Materials

Small bell findings x 8

Small thin buttons x 7

Large thin buttons x 6

Conical toggle, e.g. from tracksuit

Medium aluminium sheet, 0.032mm

Thin aluminium sheet, 0.016mm

Large button

Small domed button

Cone finding

Small wooden lice beads x 2

Medium round bead

Small round bead

Plain bell cap

Small eyelet

Small washer

Superglue

Spray primer: white

Acrylic paints: cream, yellow, red and green

Clear lacquer

Milliput

SAUCERS AND DINNER PLATES

1 Fill the thread holes of all the buttons with Milliput and smooth flat. (Fill in thread holes in the cups with Milliput at the same time.)

TEAPOT

1 Cut a triangular handle out of aluminium, with a hole this time. Glue to toggle. Cut a triangle from a snippet of thinner aluminium sheet, bend in the centre and glue opposite handle as spout.

2 Snip a tiny rectangle of aluminium and glue over the thread holes of a small button to make lid.

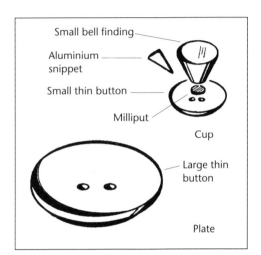

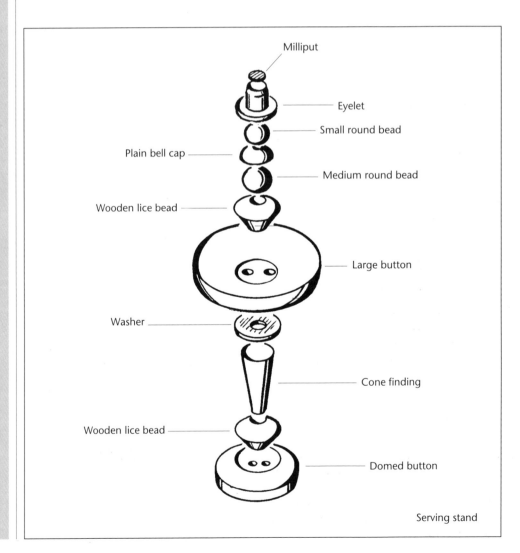

Serving stand

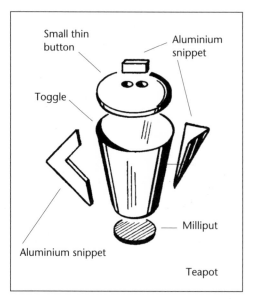

Small thin button

Aluminium snippet

Toggle

Milliput

Aluminium snippet

Teapot

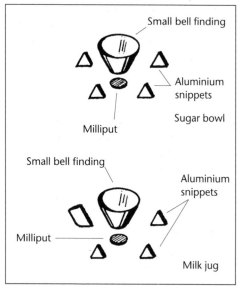

Small bell finding

Aluminium snippets

Milliput

Sugar bowl

Small bell finding

Aluminium snippets

Milliput

Milk jug

SUGAR BOWL AND MILK JUG

1 Cut several tiny equilateral triangles from aluminium strip. Select the best and glue four, evenly spaced, on the end of a bell finding. Once dry, sand base flat to ensure bowl stands level.

2 Do likewise for milk jug, but elongate one triangle to make handle. This should look similar to cup handles.

SERVING STAND

1 Glue small end of cone into a lice bead, sand end flat and glue to small, domed button. Glue other end of cone to washer.

2 Glue washer to remaining large button.

3 Glue medium round bead to lice bead. Glue plain bell cap on top, as a coat.

4 Glue small round bead to bell cap. Glue eyelet on top for a hat. Fill eyelet hole with Milliput.

FINISH

1 Spray all pieces with several thin coats of white primer. Leave to dry in between coats.

2 Paint the pattern on using acrylic paint (*see* illustration). The design is mostly straight lines – don't worry if it doesn't match exactly, hand painted ceramics are never uniform.

3 Leave paint to dry for 24 hours, then spray with clear lacquer.

CHAPTER FIFTEEN

Below Stairs

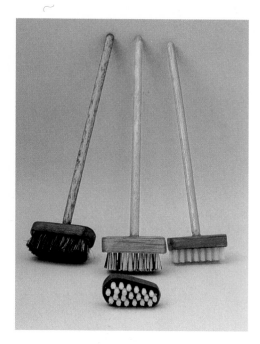

3 Glue a piece of microwood, with grain running lengthwise, to the top of the brush. Once dry, trim with manicure scissors. Blend in the veneer edges by sanding with emery board.

4 Apply a coat or two of French polish to microwood.

5 Trim bristles to size with manicure scissors.

For a used brush, distress it by gently dulling the finish a little with fine sandpaper.

BROOM

1 Using an adult's toothbrush, follow steps 1–5 above.

2 Drill a ⅛in (3.2mm) hole in the middle of broom head, at a slight angle. (Don't go through to the other side.)

3 Whittle the end of the orange stick to fit snugly into the hole. Cut the stick to size (about 4in (102mm)). Round off other end with sandpaper. Glue stick into hole with Araldite. Coat with French polish.

Materials

Toothbrushes x 2

Microwood veneer

Orange stick

Tacky glue

French polish

Araldite

Brooms and Brushes

Cleanliness was next to godliness in the Victorian opinion. The Victorians had a whole battery of brushes and brooms for every conceivable purpose. These ones are made from toothbrushes. If you want a well-used look to your brushes, use old toothbrushes.

METHOD

SCRUBBING BRUSH

1 Cut handle off toothbrush using power scissors. Sand end smooth and round off with an emery board to make head symmetrical. Roughen surface to help the veneer stick.

2 Cut a strip of microwood a little longer and wider than the side of brush. Cover sides of brush with tacky glue. (I always use glue with microwood even though it has an adhesive backing.) Press the microwood around the sides of the brush, level with the lower edge. Clamp in a vice to dry. Stick a little of the overlap down, cut off excess level with the top.

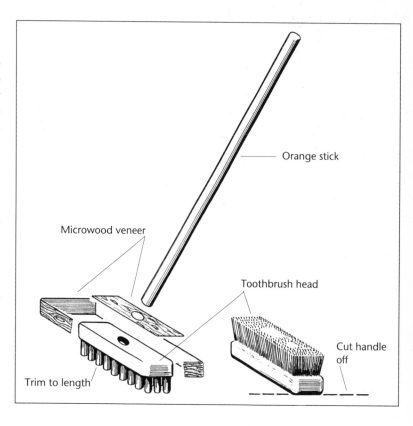

Rolling Pin and Pastry Brush

Wooden kitchen utensils don't need staining or polishing – a natural wood finish is appropriate.

METHOD

PASTRY BRUSH

1 Trim banister to about 1¹⁄₁₆in (27mm). Round off handle end with sandpaper.

2 Drill a tiny ¹⁄₃₂in (1mm) hole in the brush end. Enlarge a little with a round file.

3 Fill drill hole with glue. Press clumps of hair into hole. Leave to dry. Trim hairs level, with manicure scissors.

ROLLING PIN

1 Cut a length of dowel about 1in (25.5mm) long. Sand ends smooth.

2 Drill a central hole in each end using a tiny ¹⁄₁₆in (1.5mm) drill bit. Using drill bit as a gouge, gouge out each end so that a belaying pin can be glued in. Repeat for other handle.

Materials

Banister spindle

Hair (I used my own)

Dowel, ³⁄₁₆in (5mm)

Belaying pins x 2

Wood glue

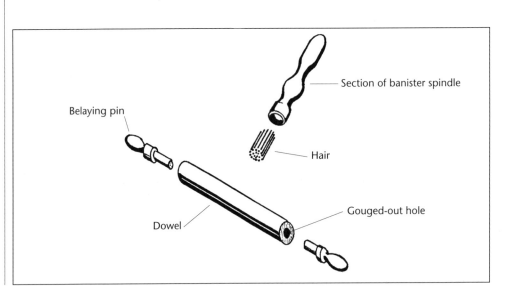

Belaying pin

Section of banister spindle

Hair

Dowel

Gouged-out hole

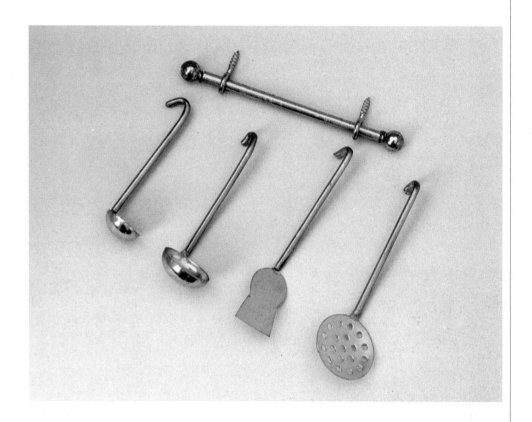

Brass Kitchen Utensils

These utensils would hang happily in any kitchen, from the eighteenth century up to the present day. For a 1930s kitchen, give the utensils several thin coats of off-white spray paint, for an enamelled effect.

If the hearth is open, make the handles a little longer. Until the arrival of the closed range, patented in 1802, the commonest cause of women's death – next to child birth – was hearth death, resulting from severe burns and shock.

Materials

Gilt sieve finding

Small gilt clawed clamp

Medium gilt clawed clamp

Round brass tube, 1/16in (1.5mm)

Round brass tube, 3/32in (2.5mm)

Brass pins x 2

Small brass screw-eyes x 2

Brass sheet, 0.005in

Araldite

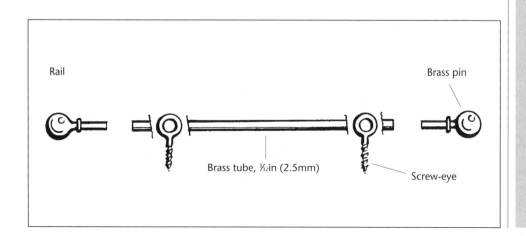

Rail

Brass pin

Brass tube, 3/32in (2.5mm)

Screw-eye

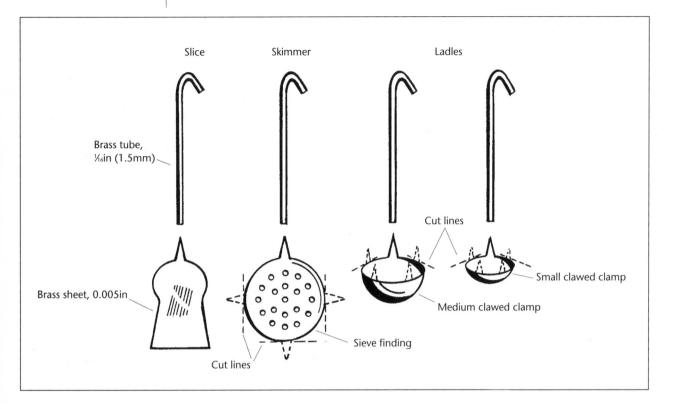

Slice   Skimmer   Ladles

Brass tube, ⅟₁₆in (1.5mm)

Brass sheet, 0.005in

Cut lines

Sieve finding

Cut lines

Small clawed clamp

Medium clawed clamp

METHOD

HANDLES

1 Mark 1⅜in (35mm) on a length of ⅟₁₆in (1.5mm) brass tube. Carefully bend end into a hook using pliers. Cut tube at the mark with metal snips. Repeat for three handles.

It is easier to bend the hook before cutting off the excess tubing.

LADLES

1 Carefully crimp one of the claws on the gilt clawed clamp so it will fit into tube handle. (File claw to shape if need be.) Snip off four remaining claws and discard. File ladle smooth.

Crimp a claw before cutting off the rest. That way you have five attempts at perfecting it. Be careful not to fatigue the metal too much, it might snap off.

SKIMMER

1 Repeat above method using sieve finding and snipping off only three claws.

SLICE

1 Use the template above to cut slice from thin brass sheet. Leave a small channel at the top to insert into the brass tube handle.

FINISHING

1 Glue the utensils into the handles. Prop them at an appropriate angle to dry.
2 Cut a 1¾in (44.5mm) length from ³⁄₃₂in (2.5mm) brass tube.
3 Fix two screw-eyes to the overmantel or wall to hold rail. Thread rail through screw-eyes.
4 Glue a brass pin into each end of tube to secure.

If you want the option of moving the rail at a later date, use Grip Wax to secure the pins rather than glue.

Preserves

When I first made miniature preserves with varnish I wondered how they would keep and whether they would leak – I have been fairly careful to keep them upright in the cupboard. Some of them must be about ten years old by now – well past their use-by date. The pickle jar is a pot which contained oil paint from a painting-by-numbers set. The rest are cut down plastic cosmetic caps.

METHOD

REDCURRANTS

1 Roll a very thin string of black Fimo. Thread into hole of a red seed bead and roll between your fingers so Fimo fills the hole. Harden in a cooling oven.

PICKLES

1 Scrape off most of the coating from tiny pearls. Leave a few specks on to look like skin.

PRUNES

1 I did go to the trouble of drying tiny berries for prunes but whole peppercorns make a much easier alternative.

LEMON CURD

1 Fill jar with a blend of transparent and yellow Fimo.

JAR

1 Using the base end, trim the plastic tube to size using a junior hacksaw. Smooth end with sandpaper.
2 Superglue plastic coated wire around the jar to make a rim.
3 Fill jar with prepared preserve.
4 Drip appropriate colour varnish over filling until it's just covered.
5 Trim down a section of cork, using a craft knife, to fit the jar snugly. If there are any gaps, fill them with slithers of cork or silicone sealant.
6 Cut a circle of cotton fabric (draw around a button).
7 Spray the circle with starch and fit over the cork. Secure tightly with thread.
8 Write name of contents on a snippet of sticky label. Cut to size and stick to jar.

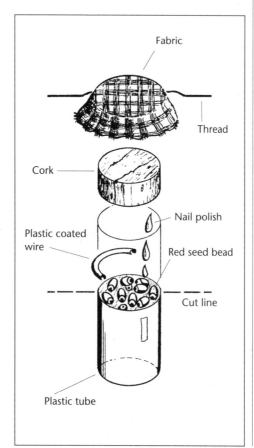

Fabric

Thread

Cork

Nail polish

Plastic coated wire

Red seed bead

Cut line

Plastic tube

Materials

Varnish: pink and brown

Cork

Plastic tubes, e.g. small cosmetic lids

Snippet of fabric

Thread

Thin, plastic coated wire

Superglue

Silicone sealant

Spray starch

Red seed beads

Fimo: black, transparent and yellow

Tiny pearls

Peppercorns

Materials

Banister spindles
(preferably square
legged) x 4

Square wood strip,
¼in (6.5mm)

Wood strip, ½in
(13mm)

Emulsion paint: white
with a hint of grey

Tacky glue

Wood strip

Square wood strip

Banister spindle

Limed Pine Table

In the last century, a mixture of wax and chalk
was used as a disinfectant to wash down
kitchen furniture and floors. This process was
called liming. It is reproduced nowadays as a
purely decorative effect. I used to create a limed
effect with ordinary white emulsion paint until
I ran out one day and had to find an alternative.
I came across a sample pot of 'white with a hint
of grey' and found it improved the effect.

METHOD

1 Trim a little from the top of all four
   banisters.
2 From the square wood strip cut two 3⅞in
   (99mm) and two 1⁹⁄₁₆in (40mm) lengths. Make
   up into a rectangle and glue a banister leg at
   each corner. Butt assembly into a jig, e.g. the
   corner of a square tray, and leave to dry.
3 Cut five strips from the ½in (13mm) wood
   strip. Glue the strips side by side and butt into
   a jig as above to ensure top dries squarely.
4 Once dry, glue leg assembly squarely onto
   underneath of table top.
5 When dry, sand smooth.
6 Use an old toothbrush to scrub table all over
   with paint, thinned down with a little water.
   Wipe off excess if necessary. Leave
   unstained and unpolished.

Meat Safe

In previous centuries meat was generally hung for a while to improve its flavour before being eaten. Well-to-do houses stored the joint in a meat safe to protect it from vermin and insects. Some meat safes had locks, but I trust my kitchen staff! The photograph shows a suitable joint of ham to hang in the safe (*see* page 49).

METHOD

1 Lightly sand all pieces of wood. Mitre all edges for a right angle fit.
2 Make and glue together two matching rectangles from cut pieces of wood strip.
3 Glue together a third rectangle for the door.
4 Glue net to inside back of the three rectangles. Pull taut before it dries then trim to size.
5 Glue together a box using the two side

Materials

Square wood strip, ⅛in (3mm)

Wood sheet, ⅛in (3mm)

Netting, e.g. tulle or plain net curtain

Soft leather

Eye from hook and eye fastener

Tiny brass nails x 2

Wood glue

Tacky glue

rectangles (covered with net) and two wood sheet rectangles as top and base. The remaining wood sheet rectangle is the back.

6 Glue a thin strip of leather to edge of both box and door to make a hinge.

7 Snip one thread hole off eye from the hook and eye fastener. Push a tiny brass nail through the remaining eye. Drill a tiny hole ½in (1mm) into side edge, opposite hinge,

and push in nail with eye.

8 Drill a similar hole into the side door, and push a second nail in, for the catch to latch onto.

9 If you wish to hang your meat safe, drill a tiny ½in (1mm) hole in the centre of the meat safe top. Thread the brass wire, attached to the ham, through the hole and bend into a hook. Hang from a screw-eye in the ceiling.

Cutting List

Sides, from ⅛in (3mm) square wood strip:
1¾in (44.5mm) x 6
1¹⁄₁₆in (27mm) x 4

Door, from ⅛in (3mm) square wood strip:
1¾in (44.5mm) x 2
1½in (38mm) x 2

Back, from ⅛in (3mm) wood sheet:
1⁵⁄₁₆ x 1⅝in
(33.5 x 41mm) x 2
1¾ x 1⅝in
(44.5 x .41mm) x 1

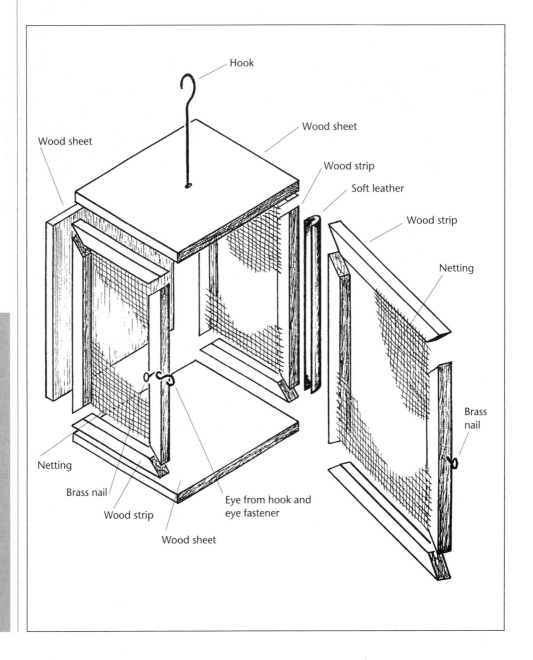

Hook

Wood sheet

Wood sheet

Wood strip

Soft leather

Wood strip

Netting

Brass nail

Netting

Brass nail

Wood strip

Wood sheet

Eye from hook and eye fastener

128

CHAPTER SIXTEEN

Hobbies and Pastimes

Sewing Box and Accessories

No Georgian or Victorian lady would have been without her sewing box. It's very easy to make an attractive one, with a decorative stand, from a pillbox and some buttons. I found this pillbox, with its embroidered top, in a flea market.

Sewing Box

METHOD

1 Glue a short length of thin cord to the lid and base of the box to prevent the lid opening beyond a right angle (*see* illustration).
2 If necessary, line your pillbox with velour or silk. My pillbox was already lined.

Sticky-back velour can often be peeled out of jewellery gift boxes.

---

3 Glue the half rivet centrally to the base of the pillbox. Leave to dry.

Araldite can discolour brass over time. Once the joint is dry, gently scrape off excess glue with the blade of a craft knife.

---

4 Cut a 1¾in (44.5mm) length of brass tube. Glue one end into the rivet on the box base. Prop up till dry.
5 Glue medium button to large button. Glue small button on top. Glue brass spacer on top of small button (*see* illustration).
6 Glue other end of brass tube into the spacer assembly. Ensure this dries upright.

Sewing Accessories

METHOD

1 To make skeins of embroidery silk, wind a single strand of thread around thick dowel, remove and secure in a hank with a snippet of black shiny paper. Add a gold line drawn on paper with a thin marker pen.
2 Straighten an old hook and eye hook to make tiny scissors.
3 Stick a few lengths of beading wire into a snippet of black paper to look like needles. Trim wires to size.

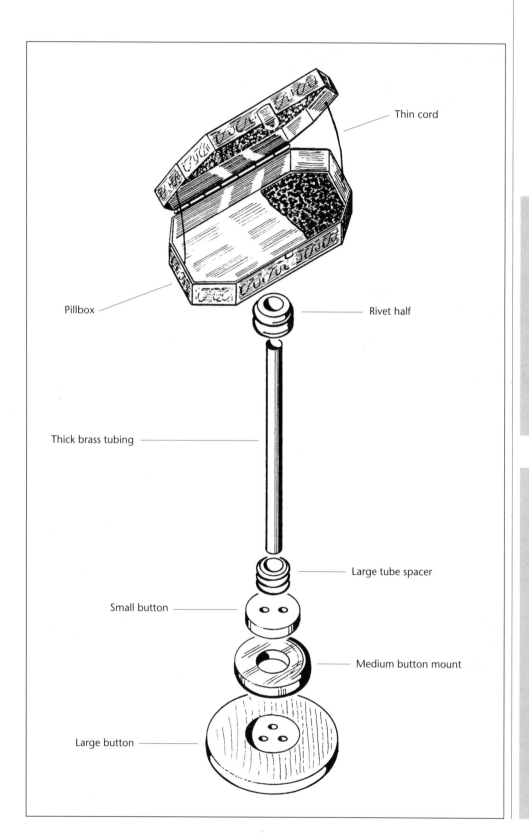

Thin cord

Pillbox

Rivet half

Thick brass tubing

Large tube spacer

Small button

Medium button mount

Large button

Materials

Sewing Accessories

Embroidery silks

Black shiny paper

Thin marker pen: gold

Hook from hook and eye fastener

Beading wire

Materials

Sewing Box

Pillbox

Thin cord

Thick brass tubing, ³⁄₁₆in (5mm)

Large brass spacer

Half a rivet

Small button

Medium button (I used a button mount minus its plastic centre)

Large button

Araldite

Egg Collection

A popular Victorian pastime was the study and collection of birds' eggs. This collection includes eggs of the guillemot, golden eagle, avocet, kestrel, jackdaw, nuthatch, and blackbird. The stand can be freestanding or mounted on a wall.

Materials

Fimo: white, brown, blue and yellow

Thin wood sheet, ⅟₁₆in (1.5mm)

Thin wood strip, ⅟₁₆in (1.5mm)

Acrylic paints: brown, black and white

Grip Wax

Wood glue

METHOD

1 Mix different shades of Fimo such as white, very pale blue, mid and light brown, beige, cream and pale yellow. Roll varying sizes of eggs with coloured Fimo. Balls of Fimo tend to alternate naturally between round and oval when rolled very lightly in the palm of the hand with a fingertip or the heel of the hand. Simply stop rolling when the ball is oval and roll onto a baking tray. Harden in a cooling oven, maximum temperature 210°F (100°C).

Vary the shapes: some birds' eggs are round, others are ovoid and some are pointed at the smaller end.

2 To speckle eggs, paint a little acrylic paint onto an old toothbrush. Flick the bristles over the egg with the point of a cocktail stick. The speckles dry almost instantly. Roll the egg over a little and repeat till covered. Speckles can be shades of brown, black, or white.

3 To make mount, cut a rectangle from wood sheet, 1 x ¹¹⁄₁₆in (25.5 x 17.5mm). Round off one of the long edges into a curve, with an emery board.

4 Glue three sections of wood strip onto the back, evenly spaced, as shelves. When dry, sand down strips from the front, to graduate the shelves in depth.

5 Glue a length of wood strip to each side (same height as back of mount) so the straight edge is flush with the back edge. Trim excess strip with power scissors. Sand sides flush with shelves with an emery board.

6 Round off top of side pieces. Coat shelves with French polish.

7 Fix eggs to shelf using Grip Wax. I finished the display with a thin coat of spray lacquer to give the eggs a sheen and encourage them to stay in place.

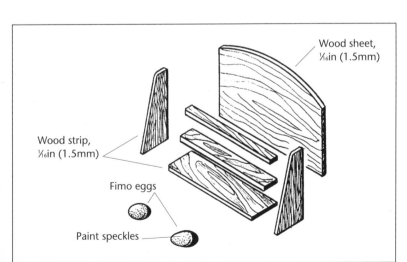

Wood sheet, ⅟₁₆in (1.5mm)

Wood strip, ⅟₁₆in (1.5mm)

Fimo eggs

Paint speckles

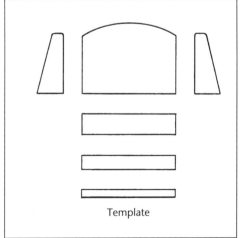

Template

Wax Fruit

This type of decoration would have appeared on the Victorian table or sideboard. It may have been fashioned by the lady or daughters of the house. Heaven forbid they should do anything remotely useful.

Wax fruit was idealized perfect fruit. The covered display, also shown in photograph, is made from Grip Wax blended with greasepaint (children's oil-based, face paint crayons). This wax fruit looks very realistic, but needs to be kept under a protective cover, e.g. plastic dome, as it attracts dust and is very easily squashed.

METHOD

BOWL

1 Glue domed button to recessed button, lining up thread holes.

CITRUS FRUITS

1 Blend orange Fimo with transparent. Roll four small balls and place on a baking tray. Carefully make an indentation on top and bottom, with a pinhead, and dot on green Fimo.

> **Blend as little coloured Fimo with transparent as will give the appropriate shade; this retains the waxy texture of transparent Fimo.**

2 Repeat for a lemon and a lime. Use yellow and green for lime and yellow and transparent for lemon. Roll each fruit at a slight angle to elongate the shape.

APPLES

1 Blend a small amount of green and transparent Fimo. Roll four small balls, press an indentation in the base with the end of a paintbrush and a smaller indentation in the top with a pinhead.

PLUMS

1 Blend purple and transparent Fimo. Roll into small ovals.

CHERRIES

1 Blend a small amount of red and transparent Fimo. Roll eight tiny balls. Cut short lengths of green florists' wire. Bend in half with pliers and stick a cherry to each end. Make four pairs.

> **When working with different shades of Fimo, rubbing a little tacky glue over your fingers is a quick way to remove colour residue.**

FINISHING

1 Harden all fruit in the oven at 210°F (100°C) for 10 minutes.
2 Arrange fruit in a pyramid shape in the bowl with a little tacky glue.
3 Coat fruit with a thin coat of clear lacquer to give a slight sheen.

Materials

Large recessed button, plastic or glass

Domed button

Fimo: orange, transparent, green, yellow, red and purple

Thin green florists' wire

Tacky glue or glass glue

Clear lacquer

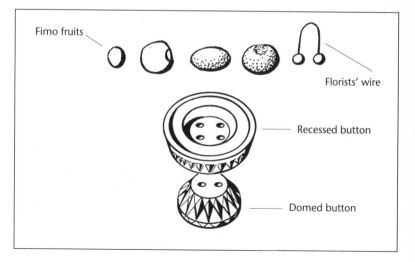

Fimo fruits

Florists' wire

Recessed button

Domed button

Lawn Bowls

Each player has his or her own set identified by a different colour ring on the ball.

METHOD

BOWLS

1 Fill the thread holes of the wooden beads with Milliput, or wood filler, and smooth off.
2 Lightly sand beads till smooth. Paint the Milliput or filler to match wood. Coat beads with several thin coats of French polish until they are smooth and shiny.
3 When dry, paint a white dot on one of the filled holes of each of the beads. Leave to dry.
4 Paint a coloured circle on the opposite end. Leave to dry.
5 Fill in thread holes of the small white bead, the Jack, with Superfine Milliput.

BOX

1 Use Blu-Tack to secure the four bowls on a corner of the wood sheet.
2 Cut four wood rectangles out of the wood sheet, to size, to make a box around the bowls. Mitre the corners. Glue to the wood base.
3 Cut box away from wood sheet with power scissors and sand sides smooth.
4 Cut thin wood strip to fit three sides of the box. Mitre the corners, glue on. Sand edges smooth.
5 Cut a wood lid from the wood sheet to fit between the wood strips. Score a half circle in the lid with a craft knife to make a hand grip.
6 Stain and coat box with a few coats of French polish.

French polish can sometimes be difficult to apply in several coats because it dries so quickly. Apply a dot of linseed oil to your brush sparingly. This will help prevent streaking.

---

7 Line inside of box with double-sided tape. Press fabric onto tape.
8 Glue corners flat and trim off excess fabric with manicure scissors.
9 Neaten top edge with a little tacky glue.

Materials

Medium wooden beads x 4

Small white bead

Wood sheet, 1⁄16in (1.5mm)

Thin wood strip or matchsticks

Snippet of thin lining material, e.g. silk

Tacky glue

Wood stain

Acrylic paint: brown, red and white

Milliput or wood filler

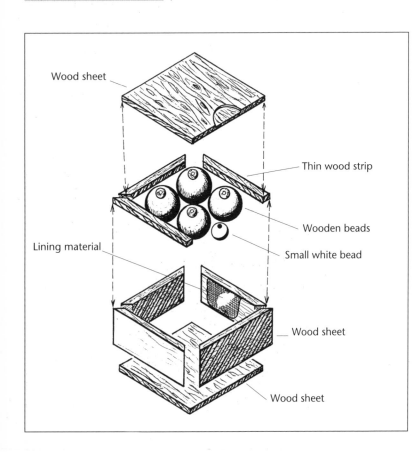

Wood sheet

Thin wood strip

Wooden beads

Small white bead

Lining material

Wood sheet

Wood sheet

Dried Flower Picture

I like to think this is the lady of the house's wedding posy, dried and preserved under glass. Look out for a suitable watch or brooch case to house the display.

METHOD

1 If the strap holders are still attached to the watchcase, remove these with pliers, then sand case smooth.

2 Draw around the case on a scrap of silk to give an approximate size for the arrangement, allowing for an overlap.

3 Arrange flower heads on silk using a T-pin dipped in a tiny amount of tacky glue.

When making a dried flower picture, make up display on plain paper first. Start with the background greenery and work to the centre, finishing with the choicest blooms in the centre.

---

4 Once the arrangement is finished, glue some false stems below the bunch.

5 Cut a cardboard backing to fit the watchcase.

6 Lay silk arrangement centrally over cardboard and stick overlap to back of card with spray mount.

7 Press watchcase onto card with winder hole at top. (It can be glued, but I prefer the option to remove if desired.)

8 Screw the screw-eye through winder hole into cardboard. To finish, tie a length of thin ribbon to screw-eye.

Materials

Selection of tiny dried flowers

Large watchcase

Scrap of silk

Thin ribbon

Card

Screw-eye

Tacky glue

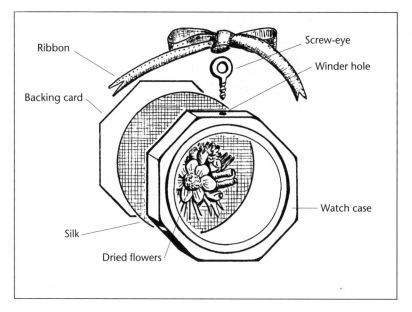

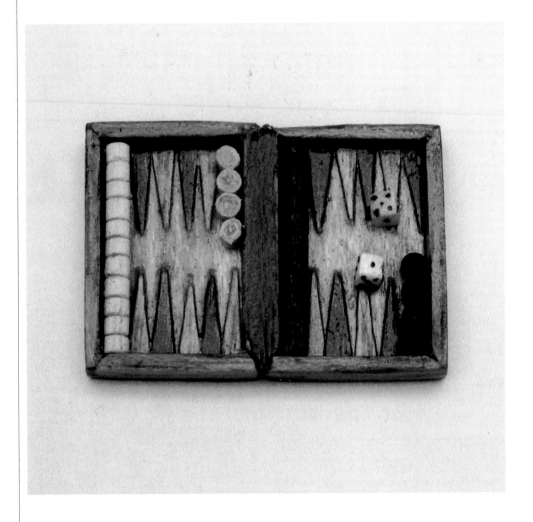

Backgammon Set

Board and card games were one of the most popular evening diversions right up until the advent of radio in the 1930s. Many board games go back to Tudor times – backgammon was a favourite of Ann Boleyn. I made this compact set from matchsticks, cocktail sticks and snippets of veneer and microwood.

METHOD

BOARD

1 Snip several thin arrow points out of pale microwood, with manicure scissors. Try to make them as small as possible, about ⁵⁄₁₆in

(8mm) long. Choose 24 thin ones of even length.

2 Colour 12 arrows black with a felt pen. Stain the remaining 12 dark brown with wood stain.

3 Stick six arrows, in alternating colours, next to each other, onto a corner of the microwood veneer.

4 Stick another six, opposite the first row, in the opposite pattern, leaving a ⅛in (3mm) gap between. (*See* view, right.) Make two such boards.

5 Frame the boards with thin wood strip, fitting closely around the patterns, and mitre the ends. Glue in place and butt into a jig to ensure these dry square.

6 Carefully cut away the excess microwood

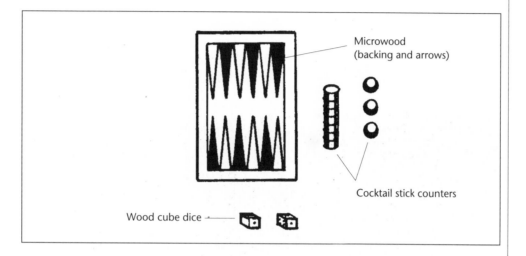

Microwood
(backing and arrows)

Cocktail stick counters

Wood cube dice

around frames with power scissors.

7 Glue a darker shade of veneer to back of the microwood bases. Lightly sand rough edges.

8 Coat the outer cases with French polish. Give the boards a thin coat of French polish to blend in the arrow veneers.

9 With the two halves of the case butted together, stick a very thin strip of leather over the sides to make a hinge.

Very thin strips of leather can be peeled carefully from the surface of soft leather but it's virtually impossible to peel off a large section.

COUNTERS

1 Mark at least 15 counters of ⅛in (3mm) along a cocktail stick.

2 Roll the cocktail stick as you gently score round the counters with a craft knife, to cut them. Glue in as many as will fit against the side of the board. Cut the leftover counters from the cocktail stick to make up to 15 and glue them to the opposite side of the board. Repeat for the black counters, staining them first with a black felt pen.

3 To make dice, cut two tiny cubes from the end of a matchstick. Sand smooth. Use a pin to make dots, dipped in black acrylic paint.

Materials

Pale microwood veneer

Thin darker wood veneer

Thin wood strip, e.g. matchsticks

Snippet of thin glove leather

Cocktail stick

Tacky glue

Felt pen: black

Acrylic paint: black

Wood stain: dark

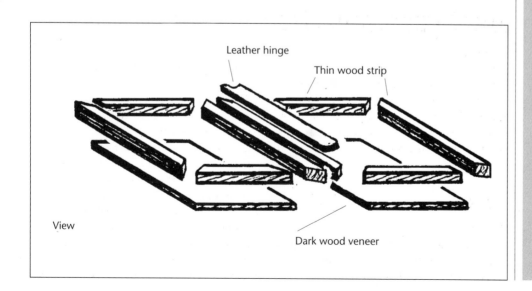

Leather hinge

Thin wood strip

View

Dark wood veneer

CHAPTER SEVENTEEN

Electrified Lighting

Oil Burning Lamp

Burning some form of oil to provide light dates back to ancient times. The lamp design changed little over the centuries and consisted of a brass, bronze or stone holder containing a wick. The decorative back to this design allows it to be wall mounted.

Washers can be found in hardware shops, but bead suppliers stock a wider range more suitable for miniature work, including metal sequin-like washers in gold and silver.

METHOD

1 File a recess in shaped washer to fit side of small thick washer. Secure in place with Blu-Tack.

I used a conical burr which you can attach to a mini drill, however, a round file will do to file a recess.

---

2 Carefully straighten one scroll on the butterfly earring back. Slightly enlarge the other scroll. Adjust to fit base of lamp. Glue thin washer over post hole of earring back.
3 Glue small thick washer into recess of shaped washer.
4 Thread bulb wires through thick washer,

Materials

Flying saucer-shaped washer (turned brass)

Small thick washer

Small thin washer

Sequin washer (from bead suppliers)

Tiny gold seed bead

Butterfly earring back

Clip-on earring back (optional)

Wired micro candle bulb, 12 volt

Grip Wax

Superglue

then through post hole and through thread hole of thin washer.

5 Carefully glue base assembly to body, concealing bulb wires between parts so that they exit through thread hole in the small thin washer.

When installing lamp, hide wires in wall or behind furniture. When the bulb needs replacing, the lamp will have to be snapped apart. (Clean old glue off with white spirit before gluing again.)

6 Glue clip-on earring back to handle. It should fit on without adjustment, but the base may need trimming slightly to allow lamp to stand.

7 To make lid, glue seed bead to thread hole of sequin washer.

8 Wash over lamp with a dilute solution of black acrylic to look like soot. Paint visible bulb wires black to resemble wick.

Smear a little Grip Wax over the candle bulb to give a more diffused glow.

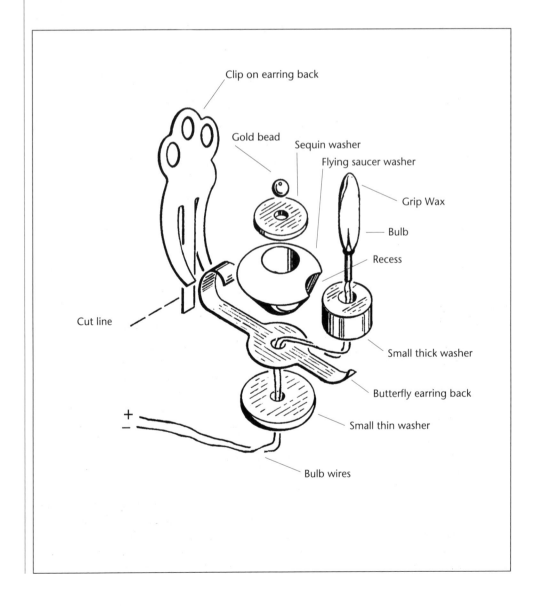

Hand Candle Lamp

A guarded candle holder, like this design from the 1800s, was a wise precaution in the nursery which, like the servants quarters, usually relied on candlelight right into the twentieth century. Don't forget to conceal the bulb wires from candle, oil and gas light in your room setting.

I find superglue suitable for this project since a good brand sticks gilt jewellery findings so well that the joint can't be dissolved even when soaked in acetone – I know, I've tried. The thin plastic tube is a section from a children's vitamin dropper.

The wiring on 12 volt wired micro bulbs is very fine. The plastic insulation coating is easily damaged while adjusting the bulb. It won't matter if one wire becomes bared, but if both bare wires touch, the bulb will short. Damaged insulation can be repaired with a smear of silicone bathroom sealant.

METHOD

BODY

1 Gently close loop on screw earring fastener. Snip off all above loop with power scissors and sand remainder smooth. (The screw part could be used for Pendant Oil Lamp: *see* page 146.) Glue handle over join on tube spacer.

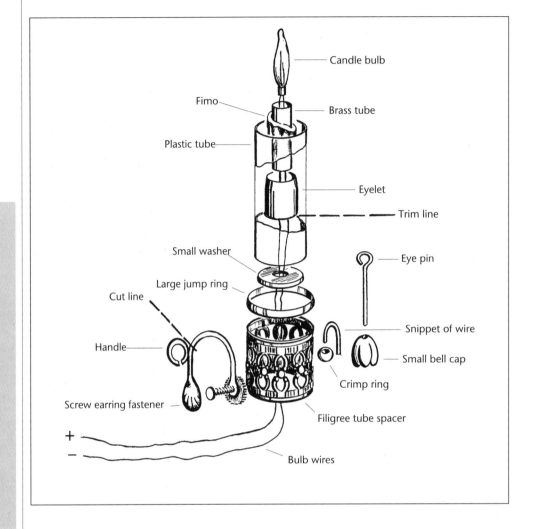

Materials

Large filigree tube spacer

Thin plastic tube to fit inside tube spacer (from a vitamin dropper or similar)

Small metal sequin washer, to fit inside plastic tube

Screw earring fastener

Crimp ring or similar

Tiny eye pin

Small tulip bell cap

Snippet of brass wire

Eyelet

³⁄₃₂in (2.5mm) brass tube

Fimo: transparent, yellow and black

Wired micro candle bulb, 12 volt

Large jump ring

Grip Wax

Superglue

SNUFFER

1 Glue crimp ring to opposite side of spacer.
2 Glue end of eye pin into small bell cap.
3 Bend a snippet of brass wire into a 'u' shape, glue one side to the bell cap. Hook other end into crimp ring and secure with a dot of Grip Wax.

GLASS COVER

1 Trim the eyelet to the same size as the washer and glue to base.
2 Trim the plastic tube to twice the height of the tube spacer. Sand the inside of the tube to fit the eyelet and washer assembly if necessary.

CANDLE

1 Blend a scrap of yellow Fimo with transparent, and add a speck of black to make a tallow colour.
2 Press a layer of Fimo tallow onto a length of ³⁄₃₂in (2.5mm) brass tubing and smooth. Roll thin Fimo strings and run down candle for drips. Harden carefully in a cooling oven.
3 Thread the bulb wires carefully through the candle, then through the hole in the eyelet and washer assembly. Fit washer into base of plastic tube.
4 Gently ease plastic tube assembly into tube spacer.
5 Push a large jump ring over the plastic tube down to the inside of tube spacer.

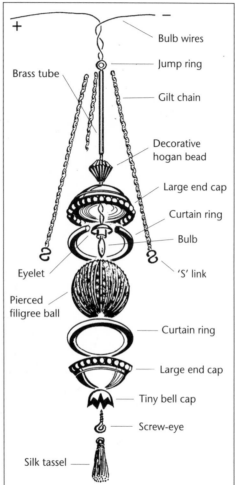

Moorish Lantern

I found this lamp design in an oriental room which appeared in the *Hampton and Sons Complete House Furnishings Catalogue* of 1894. The fashionable Victorian gentleman's den was sometimes decorated in an African or Oriental style.

METHOD

1 Thread tiny bell cap onto screw-eye. Screw into hole in one large end cap. Glue curtain ring over end cap.
2 Glue large filigree ball onto curtain ring, thread hole lengthways.
3 Glue eyelet to the inside of the remaining end cap. Thread bulb wires through eyelet and end cap hole. Thread bulb wires through hogan bead and glue bead to top of end cap. Thread wires through length of brass tube, 1¼in (32mm) long.
4 Fit bulb into thread hole of large filigree ball.

Press hole onto eyelet, which may need widening to accommodate.
5 Attach the three 's' links to the remaining curtain ring and glue to bottom of upper end cap, spacing links evenly.
6 Attach even lengths of thin chain to each link.
7 Attach other end of chain lengths to a jump ring.
8 Thread bulb wires and brass tube through jump ring and through hole in ceiling. Secure to floor above with Milliput. Secure jump ring to ceiling with Grip Wax.
9 To make tassel, thread embroidery silk through screw-eye, knot ends together and trim.

Keep a 12 volt battery handy to test bulbs before fitting.

Materials

Large end caps x 2

Large pierced filigree ball

Brass curtain rings x 2

Tiny bell cap

Screw-eye

Eyelet

Small decorative hogan bead

³⁄₃₂in (2.5mm) brass tube

Tiny gilt chain

Wired micro bulb, 12 volt

'S' shaped links x 3

Small jump ring

Silk embroidery thread

Superglue

Grip Wax

Materials

Curly gilt curtain hooks x 2

Plastic toggles x 2

Scrap of silk

Selection of seed beads

Scrap of thin cording

Brass eyelets x 2

Wired micro bulbs, 12 volt x 2

Spray mount or tacky glue

Pair of Gas Wall Lamps

Gas light was dimmer and less effective than electricity. In a Victorian house, it was more common to find several means of gas and oil lighting in a room rather than one central ceiling light.

These wall lights are styled on Edwardian gas lights, but would look equally well in a Victorian or 1920s setting. Look in charity shops for old gilt curtain hooks.

METHOD

SHADE

1 Cut a length of silk a little larger than the toggle. Spray toggle with spray mount (or smear with a thin even coat of tacky glue). Cover toggle with silk, poke excess into top hole and fold inside at base. Fold and glue overlap neatly.

2 Sew a length of thin cording around the shade base.

3 Sew a string of seven seed beads onto the cording using a fine needle and thread.

If you need to thread really tiny seed beads and don't have a thin enough needle to hand, coat the end of the thread with nail varnish. This allows the beads to thread straight on.

---

4 Thread the needle back through all but the last bead – this one keeps the others on. Sew the thread back through the same point in the cording and continue the pattern next to the first string of beads until all the cording is fringed.

Don't sew beads too tightly or closely together, the fringe should swing a little.

FITTINGS

1 Bend the straight end of the curtain hook into a curve, using pliers (*see* illustration).

2 Glue the brass eyelet into the large loop in the hook.

3 Paint the bulb wires gold. When dry, thread them through shade, then through end of hook. Follow the hook's curves with the wires, round to the eyelet. Thread wires through eyelet. Tack wires in place on the hook with a little tacky glue.

4 Drill a hole in the wall to take eyelet. Thread the wires through the hole. Fix from the back with Grip Wax and press the eyelet into the hole. Stick top of fixing to wall with a discretely placed ball of Grip Wax.

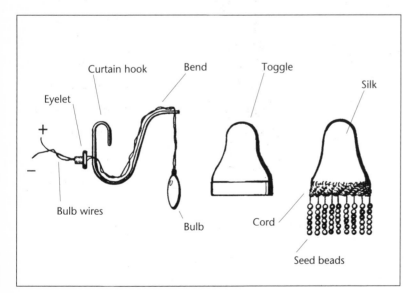

Art Nouveau Table Lamp

By the turn of the century, electric light was just appearing in a few well-to-do homes so there's no need to hide the bulb wires for this project. These lamps are based on the Art Nouveau Tiffany style. In contrast with late ornate Victoriana, the Art Nouveau style favoured naturalistic lines.

METHOD

1 Check the bulb head fits into the flower bead neatly. If not, drill out a slightly larger thread hole to take the soldered part of the bulb.
2 Cut a 1½in (38mm) length of brass tubing. Thread bulb wires through flower bead, bell cap, gold bead and brass tube. Repeat for second stem.

To thread wires through a thin tube, gently straighten the bulb wires first, thread one wire through, then follow with the second wire, a little at a time. Bulb wires will not thread through bent tubing.

---

3 Gently bend brass tubes to resemble bending stems. Using a tube bender will help to avoid kinking.
4 For base, hold the two buttons together and thread one bulb wire through each button (*see* illustration).
5 Insert one brass stem into each button hole. Glue the top button to the base button, keeping the bulb wires in place.
6 Arrange stems to twine about each other.
7 Glue gilt leaves to base.
8 Distress brass stems and leaves with a thin wash of black acrylic paint.

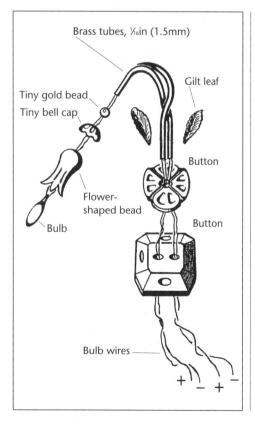

Brass tubes, ⅟₁₆in (1.5mm)

Gilt leaf

Tiny gold bead

Tiny bell cap

Button

Flower-shaped bead

Button

Bulb

Bulb wires

+ − + −

Materials

Wired micro bulbs, 12 volt x 2

Small plastic flower-shaped beads x 2

Brass tube, ⅟₁₆in (1.5mm)

Tiny bell caps x 2

Tiny gold beads x 2

Decorative buttons x 2

Small gilt leaves x 2

Superglue

Acrylic paint: black

Pendant Oil Lamp

This could be an ornate reading lamp for the sitting room. I had the idea of using tiny pressed flowers for decoration which I stuck on with transfer emulsion (*see* page 7).

METHOD

RESERVOIR

1 Glue gold bead to base of glass bead, which stands for the reservoir. Glue the smaller ends of three large scrolls, evenly spaced around the join.

The best way to get a good bond on glass-to-plastic or glass-to-metal is to tack the join together with tiny dots of superglue, then reinforce with glass glue or jewellery cement and leave to dry undisturbed.

---

2 Glue the three small scrolls at the join of the base and reservoir, between the large scrolls.
3 Snip off small end of screw fastener and glue into thread hole of bottom gold bead.
4 Glue barrel clasp half over reservoir thread hole.

SUSPENSION

1 Attach the three pierced spacers to the large jump ring. Attach a small jump ring to each end of the spacers. Attach a twisted spacer to each small jump ring. Attach an 's' link to the end of the twisted spacer.
2 Thread 's' links onto large end of large scrolls.

SHADE

1 Drill a hole in the top of the plastic capsule (if there isn't already one there).
2 Paint top and inside of rivet to match colour of shade, and varnish.
3 Glue rivet over hole in shade.
4 Decorate shade with flower patterns and varnish.
5 Bend and glue thin brass rod around base of shade, reinforcing superglue with Araldite at the join. (A curtain ring is an alternative to brass rod.)
6 Thread cotton through one seed bead, then thread both ends through another two seed beads. Thread on a short bugle bead. Smear end of the two threads with tacky glue, trim end and stick to inside of shade. Repeat, spacing evenly around shade. I used 26 strings in all.

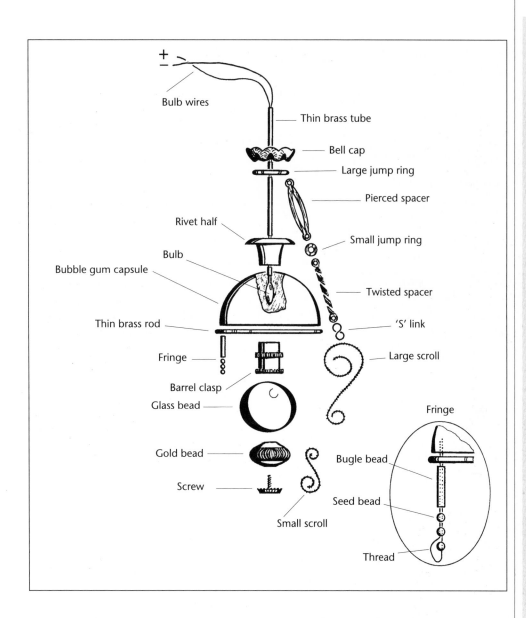

Bulb wires

Thin brass tube

Bell cap

Large jump ring

Pierced spacer

Rivet half

Small jump ring

Bulb

Bubble gum capsule

Twisted spacer

Thin brass rod

'S' link

Fringe

Large scroll

Barrel clasp

Glass bead

Gold bead

Bugle bead

Screw

Seed bead

Small scroll

Fringe

Thread

Materials

Medium glass bead

Medium gold bead

Large scrolls x 3

Small scrolls x 3

Screw from screw earring fastening

Large barrel clasp, hole half

Large jump ring

Small jump rings x 3

Twisted metal spacers x 3

Pierced spacers x 3

'S' links x 3

Half a bubble gum capsule: white

Half a large rivet

Thin brass rod, $\frac{1}{16}$in (1.5mm) or large curtain ring

Bugle beads

Seed beads

Cotton thread

Wired micro bulb, 12 volt

$\frac{3}{32}$in (2.5mm) brass tube

Pierced bell cap

Glass glue

Superglue

Araldite

Acrylic paint: white

Clear varnish

Sticky Fixer

> **To ensure fringe dangles, leave a little slack in the thread when gluing.**

HANGING

1 Thread bulb wires through a short length of thin brass tube (length will depend on how low lamp is to hang). Thread tube through hole in shade. Fix bulb into barrel clasp with Grip Wax. Thread large jump ring assembly onto tube. Thread pierced bell cap on top.

2 Glue jump ring to bell cap, spacing suspending chains evenly.

3 Thread tube through a hole in the ceiling. Fix bell cap to ceiling with a trimmed Sticky Fixer. Secure top of brass tube to ceiling with Milliput.

> **Sticky Fixers can be bought in hardware shops and stationers. They are used for securing such things as full-size mirrors to walls. They have a centre of foam and can take quite a weight, making them a strong but less permanent alternative to glue when suspending ceiling lights.**

Materials

Aluminium tube, ³⁄₃₂in (2.5mm)

Wired candle bulbs, 12 volt x 3

Eyelets x 3

Fimo: transparent, yellow and red

Thin brass wire

Tiny flower beads x 4

Seed beads x 4

Large diamond-shaped fluted filigree (can be pierced)

Vase-shaped fluted filigree

Medium cup filigree

Small scrolls x 6

Selection of tiny decorative findings

Flat filigrees x 2

Small bell cap

Tiny fluted hogan

Superglue

Jewellery cement (or Araldite)

Meissen Chandelier

Once the basic structure is made, any flower, leaf or scroll filigrees can be used to ornament this Rococo chandelier. The original has six arms, but I replaced three with tiny gilt roses since a standard transformer can only supply so many bulbs. I reinforced all the main joints with jewellery cement, and mine has survived being dropped several times.

METHOD

ARM

1 Bend a model former arm in ³⁄₃₂in (2.5mm) solid brass rod following the pattern, right, to act as a guide for shaping.

2 Thread bulb wires through the aluminium tube then carefully bend to shape with thin-nosed pliers, following the shape of the former. (Don't worry if the tube crimps a little, spray painting will disguise this.) At the end, gently bend the tube back and forth to fatigue the metal. The waste should break off easily. Bend three matching arms.

BODY

1 Drill three evenly spaced ³⁄₃₂in (2.5mm) holes in the upper half of the large diamond-shaped filigree. Thread one pair of wires from each arm through each hole, then up through the top thread hole.

2 Press an arm into each hole and secure with superglue.

3 Thread an eyelet onto each arm and glue in place halfway down vertical section of arm, as shown.

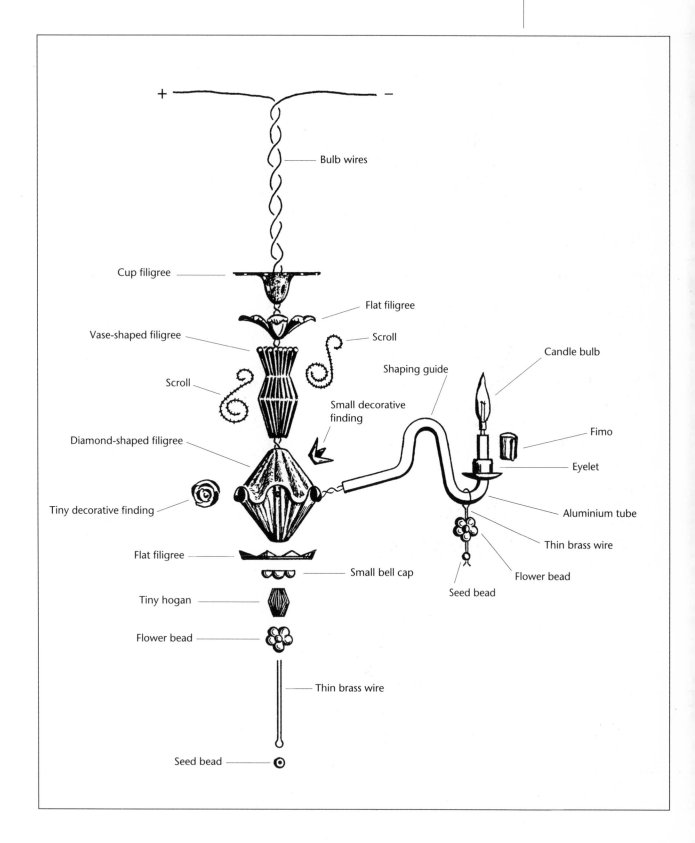

+   −

Bulb wires

Cup filigree

Flat filigree

Vase-shaped filigree

Scroll

Scroll

Shaping guide

Candle bulb

Small decorative finding

Fimo

Diamond-shaped filigree

Eyelet

Tiny decorative finding

Aluminium tube

Thin brass wire

Flat filigree

Flower bead

Small bell cap

Seed bead

Tiny hogan

Flower bead

Thin brass wire

Seed bead

4 Thread vase-shaped filigree onto bulb wires (upside down), followed by flat filigree, then medium cup filigree. Glue all pieces in place.

5 Thread a seed bead onto thin wire, fold wire and thread both ends through a flower bead, the tiny fluted hogan, the small bell cap, and through the flat filigree. Glue flat filigree and wire ends into lower thread hole of large filigree bead.

DECORATION

1 Decorate chandelier with tiny gilt filigrees. I added a rolled snippet of brass strip to make the rose centres.

2 Glue scrolls alternately around waist of vase-shaped filigree.

3 Hang thin brass wire over arm, thread on a flower bead and a seed bead. Snip off excess wire and secure with a dot of superglue in the thread hole.

When using superglue it's a good idea to have a scrap of absorbent fabric or paper to hand to soak up any excess, since this prevents the bond drying quickly.

CANDLES

1 Blend a scrap of yellow Fimo with transparent, and add a speck of red to make a colour like beeswax. Press a layer onto the aluminium tubing above the eyelet. Roll thin strings and run down candle for drips. Heat oven to 210°F (100°C), then switch off. Harden using only the residual heat of the cooling oven – the wire covering on the bulbs will melt if baked. Two sessions may be required.

2 Cover each candle and bulb with a snippet of drinking straw or similar, to protect while applying paint. Spray chandelier with several thin coats of white primer. Remove straw protectors when dry.

3 Paint decoration in bright pastels such as pink, green and orange.

4 Paint on a coat of clear gloss varnish to give a porcelain effect.

HANGING

1 Thread wires through ceiling rose. Glue top of assembly to rose. Secure rose in place with a Sticky Fixer.

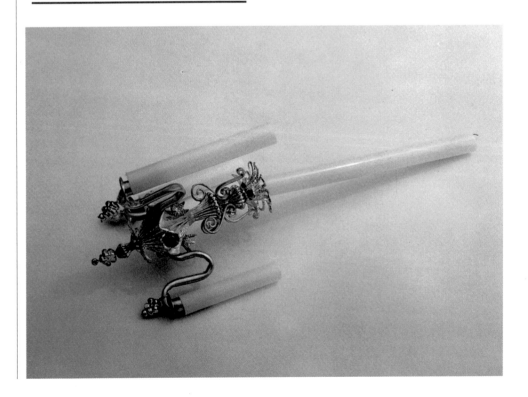

Glossary of British and American Terms

British	American
Biscuit	Cookie
Blind	Shade
Blu-Tack	Fun-tak
Bowler (hat)	Derby
Bowls	Similar to *bocce*
Braid	Embroidered trim
Budgerigar (budgie)	Parakeet
Ceiling rose	Medallion
Charity shop	Thrift shop
Clingfilm	Saran wrap
Cocktail stick	Swizzle stick
Cotton bud	Q-tip
Cotton wool (ball)	Absorbent cotton
Counterpane	Quilt or comforter
Curtains	Drapes
Drinking straw	Soda Straw
Duster	Dust cloth
Embroidery silk	DMS floss
Emulsion	Latex
Felt pen	Felt-tip pen/colored marker pen
Fish slice	Kitchen spatula
Fringe	Bangs
French polish	Furniture polish/lemon oil
Frying pan	Skillet
Greaseproof paper	Wax paper
Haberdashery	Notions
High tea	Late afternoon meal
Ironmonger	Hardware store
Lip salve	Chapstick
Lolly stick	Popsicle stick
Paraffin	Kerosene
Piping bag	Pastry bag
Rasher	Slice of bacon
Reel	Spool
Sealant (bathroom)	Caulking
Transfer	Decal
Wadding	Batting

Principal British
and American Styles

Date	British Period	American Period	Style
1485–	Henry VII	Early Colonial	Tudor
	Henry VIII		
	Edward VI		
	Mary I		
(1558)–1603	Elizabeth I		(Elizabethan)
1603–1625	James I		Jacobean
1625–1649	Charles I		Carolean
1649–1660	Commonwealth		Cromwellian
1660–	Charles II		Restoration
1689	James II		
1689–1702	William and Mary	Dutch Colonial	William and Mary
1702–1714	Queen Anne	Queen Anne	(Queen Anne)
1714–1760	Early Georgian	Chippendale	Rococo
1760–1811	Late Georgian		Neo–Classical
(1790–1810)		Early Federal	
(1798–1804)		American Directoire	Empire
(1804–1815)		American Empire	

Date	British Period	American Period	Style
1812–1830	Regency	Late Federal	Regency
1830–1837	William IV		Eclectic
1837–1901	Victorian	Victorian	
(1880–1900)			Arts and Crafts
1901–1910	Edwardian	Art Nouveau	Art Nouveau
1910–1920			
1920–1935			Art Deco

Bibliography

Abbeville Press, *Miniature Rooms: The Thorne Rooms at the Art Institute of Chicago*, The Art Institute of Chicago, Illinois, 1986

Artley, A, *Putting Back the Style*, Ward Lock Ltd, East Grinstead, 1988

Barrett, H and Phillips, J, *Suburban Style: The British Home 1840–1960*, Macdonald Orbis, London, 1987

Battersby, M, *The Decorative Twenties*, The Herbert Press, London, 1988

Clifton-Mogg, C, *The Doll's House Sourcebook*, Cassell, London, 1993

Cormack, A and Carter, D, *Flowers: Growing, Drying, Preserving*, Artists House, Mitchell Beazley Int Ltd, London, 1987

Curtis, T, *The Lyle Official Antiques Review*, 1992

De Menezes, P, *Crafts from the Countryside*, Hamlyn, London, 1981

Druitt, S, *Antique Personal Possessions to Collect*, Peerage Books, London, 1986

Edwards, R, *English Chairs*, Her Majesty's Stationery Office (HMSO), London, 1951

Farrell, J, *Umbrellas & Parasols*, Batsford Ltd, London, 1985

Gilliatt, M, *Period Decorating*, Conran Octopus Ltd, London, 1990

Guild, R, *The Complete Victorian House Book*, Sheldrake Publishing Ltd, London, 1989

Helliwell, S, *Collecting Small Silverwear*, Phaidon Christie's Ltd, Oxford, 1988

Keogh, B and Gill, M, *British Domestic Design Through the Ages*, Arthur Barker Ltd, London, 1970

Lambert, M, *Microwave Craft Magic*, The Appletree Press Ltd, Belfast, 1992

Laver, J, *Costume Through the Ages*, Thames and Hudson, London, 1963

Margetts, M, *Classic Crafts*, Conran Octopus Ltd, London, 1989

Marshall, J and Willox, I, *The Victorian House*, Sedgwick and Jackson, London, 1986

Miller, J and M, *Victorian Style*, Mitchell Beazley Int Ltd, London, 1963

Millers Antique Price Guides (various)

Ohrbach, B M, *Antiques At Home: A book of collecting and decorating with antiques*, Doubleday, London/New York, 1989

Moss, N, *The Hutchinson British-American Dictionary*, Helicon Publishing Ltd, Oxford, 1994

Nisbett, J, *The Secrets of the Dolls' House Makers*, Guild of Master Craftsman Publications Ltd, Lewes, 1994

Osband, L, *Victorian House Style*, David and Charles, Newton Abbot, 1991

Parker, F, *Victorian Embroidery*, Anaya Publishers Ltd, London, 1990

Potter, M and A, *Interiors*, John Murray Ltd, London, 1957

Ruble, A, *Through The Looking Glass: Collections in Miniature*, Boynton and Associates Inc, Clifton, Virginia, 1984

Seymour J, *Forgotten Household Crafts*, Guild Publishing, London, 1987

Wissinger, J, *Victorian Details: Enhancing Antique and Contemporary Homes with Period Accents*, Virgin, London, 1990

Wright, L, *Warm and Snug: The History of the Bed*, Routledge & Kegan Paul, London, 1962

Metric Conversion Table

inches	mm	cm	inches	cm	inches	cm
Inches to millimetres and centimetres mm = millimetres cm = centimetres							
⅛	3	0.3	9	22.9	30	76.2
¼	6	0.6	10	25.4	31	78.7
⅜	10	1.0	11	27.9	32	81.3
½	13	1.3	12	30.5	33	83.8
⅝	16	1.6	13	33.0	34	86.4
¾	19	1.9	14	35.6	35	88.9
⅞	22	2.2	15	38.1	36	91.4
1	25	2.5	16	40.6	37	94.0
1¼	32	3.2	17	43.2	38	96.5
1½	38	3.8	18	45.7	39	99.1
1¾	44	4.4	19	48.3	40	101.6
2	51	5.1	20	50.8	41	104.1
2½	64	6.4	21	53.3	42	106.7
3	76	7.6	22	55.9	43	109.2
3½	89	8.9	23	58.4	44	111.8
4	102	10.2	24	61.0	45	114.3
4½	114	11.4	25	63.5	46	116.8
5	127	12.7	26	66.0	47	119.4
6	152	15.2	27	68.6	48	121.9
7	178	17.8	28	71.1	49	124.5
8	203	20.3	29	73.7	50	127.0

Index

About the Author

Andrea has been busy making dolls' house accessories for as long as she can remember. She has now amassed a large collection of 1/12 scale accessories, many of which have a story to tell about their origins and history.

Originally trained as a beauty therapist, she now combines her lifelong passion for fashioning beautiful miniatures with a writing career. She writes for *Dolls' House World* magazine, as well as contributing to various health and beauty publications. The fruits of her work can be seen here as well as in her first book, *Easy To Make Dolls' House Accessories*.

Andrea lives with her husband Andy, a computer systems analyst, in Essex.

Titles available from
Guild of Master Craftsman Publications
Books

The Art of the Woodcarver *GMC Publications*

Carving Birds and Beasts *GMC Publications*

Carving Power Tools, Vices and Benches *GMC Publications*

Faceplate Turning: Features, Projects, Practice *GMC Publications*

Practical Tips for Turners and Carvers *GMC Publications*

Practical Tips for Woodturners *GMC Publications*

Projects and Techniques for Beginners *GMC Publications*

Spindle Turning *GMC Publications*

Useful Woodturning Projects *GMC Publications*

Woodturning Techniques *GMC Publications*

Woodworkers' Career and Educational Source Book *GMC Publications*

Woodworking Plans and Projects *GMC Publications*

40 More Woodworking Plans and Projects *GMC Publications*

Green Woodwork *Mike Abbott*

I Have Designs on You *Pat Ashforth and Steve Plummer*

I Have The Measure of You *Pat Ashforth and Steve Plummer*

Easy to Make Dolls' House Accessories *Andrea Barham*

Making Little Boxes from Wood *John Bennett*

Woodturning Masterclass *Tony Boase*

Furniture Restoration and Repair for Beginners *Kevin Jan Bonner*

Furniture Restoration *Kevin Jan Bonner*

Woodturning Jewellery *Hilary Bowen*

The Incredible Router *Jeremy Broun*

Electric Woodwork *Jeremy Broun*

Woodcarving: A Complete Course *Ron Butterfield*

Making Fine Furniture: Projects *Tom Darby*

Restoring Rocking Horses *Clive Green and Anthony Dew*

Make Your Own Dolls' House Furniture *Maurice Harper*

Embroidery Tips and Hints *Harold Hayes*

Seat Weaving *Ricky Holdstock*

Multi-Centre Woodturning *Ray Hopper*

Complete Woodfinishing *Ian Hosker*

Woodfinishing Handbook *Ian Hosker*

Woodturning: A Source Book of Shapes *John Hunnex*

Illustrated Woodturning Techniques *John Hunnex*

Making Shaker Furniture *Barry Jackson*

Upholstery: A Complete Course *David James*

Upholstery Techniques and Projects *David James*

The Upholsterer's Pocket Reference Book *David James*

Designing and Making Wooden Toys *Terry Kelly*

Making Dolls' House Furniture *Patricia King*

Making Victorian Dolls' House Furniture *Patricia King*

Making and Modifying Woodworking Tools *Jim Kingshott*

The Workshop *Jim Kingshott*

Sharpening: The Complete Guide *Jim Kingshott*

Sharpening Pocket Reference Book *Jim Kingshott*

Turning Wooden Toys *Terry Lawrence*

Making Board, Peg and Dice Games *Jeff and Jennie Loader*

Making Wooden Toys and Games *Jeff and Jennie Loader*

Bert Marsh: Woodturner *Bert Marsh*

The Complete Dolls' House Book *Jean Nisbett*

The Secrets of the Dolls' House Makers *Jean Nisbett*

Wildfowl Carving, Volume 1 *Jim Pearce*

Wildfowl Carving, Volume 2 *Jim Pearce*

Architecture for Dolls' Houses *Joyce Percival*

Make Money from Woodturning *Ann & Bob Phillips*

The Complete Pyrography *Stephen Poole*

Woodcarving Tools, Materials and Equipment *Chris Pye*

Carving on Turning *Chris Pye*

Tatting Collage *Lindsay Rogers*

Cross Stitch On Colour *Sheena Rogers*

Making Tudor Dolls' Houses *Derek Rowbottom*

Making Georgian Dolls' Houses *Derek Rowbottom*

Making Period Dolls' House Furniture *Derek & Sheila Rowbottom*

Woodturning: A Foundation Course *Keith Rowley*

Turning Miniatures in Wood *John Sainsbury*

Colouring Wood for Woodturners *Jan Sanders*

Pleasure and Profit from Woodturning *Reg Sherwin*

Making Unusual Miniatures *Graham Spalding*

Woodturning Wizardry *David Springett*

Adventures in Woodturning *David Springett*

Carving Realistic Birds *David Tippey*

Furniture Projects *Rod Wales*

Decorative Woodcarving *Jeremy Williams*

Videos

Dennis White Teaches Woodturning

      Part 1 Turning Between Centres

      Part 2 Turning Bowls

      Part 3 Boxes, Goblets and Screw Threads

      Part 4 Novelties and Projects

      Part 5 Classic Profiles

      Part 6 Twists and Advanced Turning

John Jordan Bowl Turning

John Jordan Hollow Turning

Jim Kingshott Sharpening the Professional Way

Jim Kingshott Sharpening Turning and Carving Tools

Ray Gonzalez Carving a Figure: The Female Form

David James The Traditional Upholstery Workshop

      Part I: Drop-in and Pinstuffed Seats

David James The Traditional Upholstery Workshop

      Part II: Stuffover Upholstery

GMC Publications regularly produces new books and videos on a wide range of woodworking and craft subjects, and an increasing number of specialist magazines, all available on subscription:

Magazines

Woodturning   Woodcarving   Business matters

All these publications are available through bookshops and newsagents, or may be ordered by post from the publishers at Castle Place, 166 High Street, Lewes, East Sussex BN7 1XU, Telephone (01273) 477374, Fax (01273) 478606

Credit card orders are accepted

PLEASE WRITE OR PHONE FOR A FREE CATALOGUE